Ex-Library: Friends of
Lake County Public Library

the Godfile

10 Approaches to Personalizing Prayer

by

ARYEH BEN DAVID

∞

LAKE COUNTY PUBLIC LIBRARY

Also by Aryeh Ben David:

Around the Shabbat Table:
A Guide to Fulfilling and Meaningful
Shabbat Table Conversations

3 3113 02607 0617

The Godfile: 10 Approaches to Personalizing Prayer
Published by Devora Publishing Company
Text Copyright © 2007 by Aryeh Ben David
COVER DESIGN: Batya Rubinstein
TYPESETTING: Jerusalem Typesetting
EDITOR: Sorelle Weinstein

All rights reserved. No part of this book may be used or reproduced or transmitted in any form or by any means, electronic or mechanical, including photocopying, recording, or by any information storage and retrieval system, without written permission in writing from the publisher.

Hard Cover ISBN: 978-1-932687-93-4
Soft Cover ISBN: 978-1-932687-94-1

E-mail: publisher@devorapublishing.com
Web Site: www.devorapublishing.com
Printed in the United States of America

❧

This book is dedicated to my father-in-law, Ben Shanker.
In gratitude for your modeling a life of personal
integrity, gentle kindness and acts of giving.
Your belief in the sanctity of this world
and your desire to live in the Image of God
have inspired us all to become better people.

❧

Acknowledgments

This book took many years to write. Each step that I took on my own path caused me to evaluate and reformulate ideas written during an earlier stage. I will be forever indebted to Yehoshua Rubin, Zvi Hirschfield and Rabbi Avraham Sutton. Their friendship, guidance and encouragement have immeasurably aided my spiritual journey.

For several years, Yehoshua and I had been learning together on Thursday nights. One evening, we came to the realization that despite our unwavering routine of learning, we were not growing on a personal level, and were in need of a spiritual guide. Two days later, a former student called me to ask if Pardes was looking for a new teacher. She knew of a wonderful rabbi, Avraham Sutton. I told her that although Pardes wasn't looking for more staff, I would be very interested in meeting him. The next week found Yehoshua and myself learning with Rabbi Avraham. For me, it was more of a journey than a class. Once a week for two years, in a cold, bare, synagogue in Geula, Jerusalem, we learned mystical sources, sang, meditated and contemplated our lives together. Yehoshua and Rabbi Avraham were more than just colleagues and friends; their deep trust and openness created sacred space, which, as a result, opened up new worlds for me.

Zvi Hirschfield has been my sounding board for many years. We have shared countless hours analyzing pedagogic technique and contemplating new approaches, as well as teaching and hiking together. Zvi has always had a prescient sense of the next step in our spiritual path. His friendship, keen insights, sage advice and much needed humor have deeply enriched my soul and given me greater clarity in my life.

I am a teacher, not a writer. If this book is readable, it is due to the students, friends and professional editors who thoughtfully shared with me their suggestions and gave generously of their expertise. Their comments can be felt throughout the book. Jessica Lissy, Natalie Blitt, Nomi Michlin, Jonas Rosenbloom and Yona Israel, students studying at the Pardes Institute, helped read through the initial drafts. Hanna Koppel edited the book and encouraged me to continue with this project. My friend and neighbor, David Kahn, always generated creative ideas and wholeheartedly offered his support. Ilene Prusher offered so much time and advice, I feel as if she were the one who gave life to the pages within. I gave Bob Bleiweiss, mentor and friend for over 25 years, a red pen to make a few comments. I never expected that he would devote himself so seriously to the project and make so many corrections that he used up all of its ink. Bob reviewed every page of the near-final draft and reworked major sections. I am deeply grateful for his unwavering friendship and insight. Our longtime friend, Noga Fischer, gave most generously of her time and wisdom. Sorelle Weinstein brought the book to its final copy. Her insights and professionalism transformed even the final draft. Batya Rubinstein designed the covers with a profound beauty. Her grace and professionalism was a calming presence throughout this project.

From the beginning of this book, before a single word had been written, it was my hope that the spiritual portraits of Debbi Cooper would grace this book. More than simply a photographer, my wife and I cherish Debbi's deep wisdom, trust and priceless friendship.

I am grateful for the privilege of having taught at two extraordinary institutions in Jerusalem, the Pardes Institute and Livnot U'Lehibanot. Many of the ideas mentioned in this book were conceived and taught within their walls. The intellectual rigor of the students at Pardes challenged my mind; the warmth and collegiality of the Livnot staff opened my heart. I am indebted to both institutions for helping me personally, and for the invaluable service they provide for the Jewish people.

Since 1994, my family has been blessed to live in the Barkan neighborhood of Efrat. The neighborhood's physical beauty is only surpassed by the inner beauty of our friends and neighbors. Often, people have to travel great distances to learn from inspiring personalities. I am grateful and blessed that I need only walk out my front door to be in the presence of such worthy individuals.

Most of all, I want to thank my children, Shachar, Ma'ayan, Amichai, Yaniv, Ra'aya and Lilach for being patient with their father during the countless hours he sat in front of his computer. Their purity, vitality and commitment to the Jewish people fill me with great hope for the future.

And finally, to my wife and friend, Sandra, who, with a deep breath and a courageous spirit, has walked with me along the winding, unpredictable, occasionally tortuous, but always hopeful path for the last 25 years. I could not have taken the first step without her.

Contents

Introduction: My Path

Each individual has a unique spiritual path to walk. This was not always clear to me.

Growing up, I did not give spirituality much thought. I was blessed to grow up in a warm and supportive family environment. As for our Jewish life, my family belonged to a Reform temple, and I attended Sunday school throughout most of my youth. Though not observant, we possessed strong social and cultural Jewish identities, and Judaism was an important part of our lives.

In high school, most of my time was focused on football and baseball. With the exception of pursuing a cute girl at temple youth group events, Judaism had all but disappeared from my life. Once in college, where I studied psychology, I explored the world of liberal arts. Many of my friends were religious Christians. We attended ecumenical services offered by the college, drank a lot of herbal tea, and stayed up until the early hours playing folk music, dreaming great dreams, and pondering what we were going to do with our lives.

Toward the end of my college years, I became more curious about Judaism. The rabbi of our temple had been active in the civil rights movement, and his idealism instilled in me a desire to change the world. When the time came to select a subject for an advanced degree, I vacillated between psychology and religion, and finally chose to follow in my rabbi's footsteps and become a Reform rabbi. This led me to Israel.

There, for the first time in my life, I tasted and experienced a depth within Judaism that opened up new worlds to me. I spent countless hours in the Old City, wandering slowly through the different quarters and sitting in awe near the Western Wall. I stayed up late with friends, wrestling with difficult issues: tradition vs. modernity, peoplehood vs. individuality, single truth vs. pluralism.

It was in Israel that I experienced my first Shabbat. I was invited to a family's home. It was Friday afternoon and the parents and children were frantically rushing to finish cleaning the apartment before sundown. Then, in a flash, a heavenly calm descended upon the household, and the mother lit candles to welcome Shabbat into her home. Shortly after that transformative experience, I began to experiment with observing Shabbat.

If I had to do it over again, I would do it much differently. I was on a path without a tour guide. No one in my family supported the journey. No one identified with my questions. People told me that I was throwing my life away. Then, I had always made my family and friends "proud," fulfilling their expectations by excelling in high school, going straight to college and starting on the road towards a successful career. For the first time in my life, I was following my heart and not my head, and this was difficult for the people closest to me to accept. I was expected to provide them with answers, but all I really had were questions – in fact, the biggest questions. Because I was ill-equipped to counter their skepticism, I often reacted defensively, unwilling to admit my doubts for fear that I would be left too exposed and vulnerable. Looking back, I would say that I couldn't even admit my doubts, insecurities and fears to myself. But one thing was clear: in order to become a Jewish educator and rabbi, my first step must be to accept that I needed to begin learning.

Thus began my journey into Jewish learning. For the first several years, I studied in English-speaking programs in Jerusalem. Afterwards, my wife and I moved to an all-Israeli, Hebrew-speaking yeshiva outside of Jerusalem, where we lived for four years. Although this move was not significant geographically, it was a huge leap into the unknown. Everyone else at the yeshiva had grown up in traditional homes. As time passed, we began to adopt a more traditional Jewish lifestyle, at least on an external level. We worked together to build a Shabbat-observant, kosher home, and over time, I even began to look the part. I let my beard grow long, began to wear white shirts, and walked the streets in sandals with socks. We were careful to learn and practice even the smallest details of Jewish law.

Although these were exciting and challenging years of personal growth and religious exploration, I was not concerned with the spiritual aspects of Judaism. In fact, I am not even sure that I felt I was on, or supposed to be on, a spiritual path. I did not consider myself a spiritual person. While Jewish learning absorbed me intellectually and Jewish practices intrigued me, questions of spirituality such as "What is your relationship with God? What do you mean when you say you believe in God?" never surfaced. Questions about God were not raised – not by me, and not by my yeshiva.

Finally, at the age of thirty and married with two children, I embarked on the path to become a traditional rabbi. During this period, we lived on the premises of the yeshiva, and I studied from 4:15 A.M. until late at night. However, my colleagues and I rarely broached the topic of God or spirituality, and my rabbis and teachers assumed that we had no doubts or questions about God. They assumed that we were learning in order to deepen a belief that was already firmly in place. What exactly belief in God was or might be remained a mystery to me. I certainly could not have articulated it and we did not discuss it. As a result, seeds of confusion took root within of me.

It took me years to admit that I didn't know what I believed. I had no idea how I was supposed to relate to a transcendent Being. I am not sure what triggered this realization. Perhaps after years of repressing these issues, I could no longer contain them. Or perhaps I finally felt comfortable enough with my new lifestyle to voice these doubts to myself.

In my third year at the yeshiva I reached a turning point. Suddenly, I felt that I had to talk with the rosh yeshiva (head of the yeshiva) about God. After years of religious learning and observance, I was suddenly afloat on uncharted waters. The entire foundation of my religious identity seemed to be crumbling. I felt that I had to begin all over again.

I experienced a profound state of loneliness. Was I the only person to ever have felt this way? Was I some kind of religious mutation? Was this lacuna due to a step that I had missed while making my religious leap? Was everyone else comfortably standing on a bedrock of faith?

There I was, utterly unsure of my inner religious identity. After years of living in a kind of spiritual denial, I finally had a religious breakdown. I wanted to ask others: "What exactly characterizes a relationship with God? What do you believe in?" But who talks about these things? Where could I go to work through my confusion?

I met the rosh yeshiva at his home. We sat very close to each other. I admitted to him that I was not sure if I believed in God. He just stared at me in bewilderment, and said in disbelief, "But of course you believe in God! You have been studying here for years and living a religious lifestyle. You run the minyan! How could you not believe in God?"

The rosh yeshiva was a man of great faith. Although he could not identify with or help me solve my dilemma, he generously offered me the opportunity to remain at the yeshiva until I could find some clarity.

From that day on, the focus of my learning expanded to include my spiritual quest. Instead of studying only Talmud and Jewish law, I began also to learn more philosophical and mystical texts. Beyond asking, "What does this mean and how should I behave?" I began to ask "What does Judaism believe in? How do these texts influence my relationship with God and my soul?"

As a result, I experienced a transformation that still infuses my teaching. Beyond approaching the traditional texts from an exclusively intellectual standpoint, I also began working to incorporate the learning into my innermost life, my spiritual self.

In my life, I have walked my own spiritual path. I firmly believe that each and every person has a unique spiritual path to walk. Discovering this path is a demanding challenge fraught with personal struggles. Nevertheless, if we are to gain access to our inner spiritual life and create an authentic relationship with the Divine, we have no other alternative but to embrace this challenge.

I began asking questions about God in my thirties. Twenty years later, I find myself farther along this endless path, with new spiritual questions continuously emerging. Now I am no longer intimidated by feelings of doubt, and welcome the challenge of uncertainty.

My hope is that this book will assist you in finding your own spiritual path.

How to Use the Ideas
and Practices in This Book

For individual readers – Create a computer file entitled "The Godfile." Write a paragraph or two every day in which you express some of your reflections after a Spiritual Check-up. Describe spiritual moments you have experienced.

Experiment with the ten approaches (described later in the book) one by one. Try adopting each approach for a few days or a week at a time. Each one possesses an element of truth and may be helpful at different times. Several minutes of focus on any one of these ideas can transform the entire experience of prayer. In fact, many people have found that experimenting with these approaches has led to a natural incorporation of meaningful prayer into their daily life.

You can also pair yourself with a "spiritual partner" and try out one of the approaches together. You will probably need at least one week to enter fully into the mindset. Afterwards, discuss together what worked and what was helpful. If you do not have a spiritual partner, a second-best option is to keep a journal of your thoughts as you move through the process.

For synagogues, schools and groups – Form a "*Tefilla* (prayer) group" in the same way that you would start a book club. (For more information and materials on starting a book club based on The Godfile, please visit www.ayeka.org.il.) Organize a group of people – ten would be a good number. Gathering in this forum is a great way to get to know each other. Although people talk about so many topics, prayer is rarely on the agenda. If just ten people gather regularly to discuss their relationship with God and their world of prayer, the ripples created can dramatically alter and reinvigorate the spiritual life of the entire congregation.

Try experimenting with these approaches before regular prayer services. Rabbis and school principals that begin taking just a few minutes before launching into the service report a transformation of the prayer experience. Afterwards, if possible, take time to discuss the effect of the approaches on the group's experience.

Create a safe space in which everyone can express his or her true feelings without worrying about being judged by others. From the outset, establish guidelines of confidentiality – the stricter the confidentiality. The more likely it is that people will feel secure enough to open up and share their inner lives. Just talking about a prayer frequently deepens its effect.

Once the group's rapport has been established, organize a spiritual retreat that features spiritual workshops and plenty of time for sharing spiritual moments.

For different religions – Since my primary experience in the world of prayer has been within Jewish settings, this book draws from the wisdom of Jewish sources and thinkers. However, the suggestions and approaches presented here are appropriate for readers of other religious backgrounds – especially religions that adhere to a fixed, organized liturgy. I believe that anyone seeking more personal and meaningful prayer will benefit from the ideas and suggested practices presented in the following pages.

PART I:
The Godfile

Personalizing
Our Prayer Experience

Blessed are You, Lord, *our God and the God of our Fathers,* the God of Abraham, the God of Isaac, and the God of Jacob.
     – prayer book, opening words of the Amida prayer.

The peak moment of Jewish prayer, the standing, silent prayer (the *Amida*), teaches us the primacy of personalizing the prayer experience.

The *Amida* begins with the phrase "Our God and the God of our Fathers." These are two radically different experiences of the Divine.

"Our God" reflects the God of personal experience, the God of our lifetime. "Our God" refers to our personal and private relationship with God, which is unmediated by anyone else. No one else can create this for us. No one else can teach it to us. It is intimate and uniquely ours. This close, individual connection with God is sometimes referred to as a "vertical experience," a direct encounter with the beyond. The Rabbis say that at Mount Sinai everyone heard a different voice – each person's relationship with God was unique.

"The God of our Fathers" is totally different. "The God

of our Fathers" reflects the God of history. It is the God of Abraham, Isaac and Jacob. But it is not only the God of these three forefathers. It can also be understood to include all the people that preceded us. Everyone experiences God differently. This is the path that others have walked and that we can learn from. This experience of God is not accessed directly, nor is it the product of personal experience. Rather, it is learned through texts, stories, and a tradition conveyed by others. This indirect, mediated connection with God is sometimes referred to as a "horizontal experience," which is passed on through people, rather than through a direct experience with the transcendent.

We might have thought that the *Amida* would have begun with "the God of our Fathers" and then afterward mention "Our God." Their experience chronologically preceded our own. Nevertheless, we begin the *Amida* with "Our God." "*Our* God" precedes "the God of *our Fathers.*"

Why?

First, we need to establish our own relationship with God. We need the "vertical" before the "horizontal." Only after this personal connection has been created can the teachings of "the God of our Fathers" resonate within us. The experience that others have had with God is meaningful only when we have already established our own experience of the holy.

Once in the classroom I asked if my students had ever been in love. One shook his head, saying "Never been." I said to him, "I love my wife very much. Do you have any idea how much I love my wife?" He answered, "No, not really, but it sounds nice." Since he had never been in love, he really had no idea what I was talking about. Then I asked a different student who *had* been in love before, "Do you have any idea how much I love my wife?" He nodded in confirmation and said, "Sure, I'm in love right now." Even though our experiences were probably completely different, he nevertheless could identify with my feelings and we were able to carry on a discussion from a common platform.

Only after someone has undergone a similar experience is it possible to fully identify and integrate the lessons from someone else's life. Otherwise, their experience will remain on a superficial level – that is, purely as intellectual information, that does not affect a person deeply.

This is why "Our God" has to precede "the God of our Fathers." Only *after* we have had our own direct experience with God can we then benefit from someone else's experience of the Divine. Only *after* we have had our very own uniquely personal and distinct "spiritual" experience can we identify with, and take in, the experience of someone else.

This is one of the reasons why the words of the prayerbook often do not resonate with people. They are the words of "our Fathers." They will only resonate with us after we have formed our own personal relationship with God.

Structure of this book:

The two parts of this book reflect these two experiences of "Our God" and "the God of our Fathers."

Part i – The Godfile – provides a system and tools to help us develop our own personal, unmediated relationship with God: "Our God."

Part ii – Clicking up the Godfile – introduces us to ten different approaches to prayer developed in the last 200 years of Jewish history: "The God of our Fathers."

The Godfile

To develop your relationship with God, you have to click up your Godfile. To click it up, you first have to write it.

What is a "Godfile"? The Godfile encompasses your relationship with God. It includes moments of overwhelming joy and of deep despair, of loving closeness and of painful distance. It consists of times when we are in dialogue with God and our belief is intact, and of times when we sorely feel an absence. Imagine now that all of the dimensions of this multi-faceted relationship have been transcribed to a computer file entitled "The Godfile."

Why might this metaphor be helpful? So often I have observed the frustration and disappointment of family members, friends and students – and certainly within myself as well – when the spiritual "lift" we expect at certain moments simply does not happen. Much of this frustration can be attributed to our mistaken expectations. We cannot expect to feel spiritually uplifted simply because of the uniqueness of the moment; we need to prepare ourselves in advance.

A personal example: When my wife and I were married in Jerusalem, my grandmother came to Israel for the first time for the wedding. She had been raised in a marginally connected

Jewish home, and Judaism was not central to her life. We went to the Western Wall together, where she said: "Aryeh, I'm here at the Wall for the first time and it is not doing anything for me. I don't feel anything special."

Why didn't the Wall do anything for my grandmother? I believe it is because she had not written her "Western Wall file" during her life. She had not come to Israel prepared for this potentially inspiring moment. Had she learned about this religiously significant and historical site and contemplated its meaning deeply, her visit might have been transformed into an overwhelmingly powerful experience:

Another example from routine, everyday life.

I am busy at work. In the middle of the day, I decide to call home to check in with my wife. Is it possible for us to have a brief, yet meaningful, interaction during a two or three-minute phone call? What of any consequence could possibly be expressed in these few minutes? The truth is that the amount of time is irrelevant. Even the briefest conversation offers the potential for a deep connection that is unrelated to the specific words that we will say. The conversation can be extremely meaningful and significant because over the past 25 years I have been developing and deepening my relationship with my wife, writing the "wife-file." The phone call itself will never *create* the beauty and depth of the relationship, but it can *maintain* it. This fleeting conversation is a chance to click on the wife-file in the computer of my life, briefly calling up our shared history and reinforcing our commitment to a shared future.

Clearly, the conversation will only be as meaningful as the extent of the "file." I cannot create a relationship during a two-minute phone call, but I can build on the 20-year relationship that has already been developed and sustained. This history will imbue meaning to the conversation. "I love you, Sandra."

four short words carry with them all the connections, experiences and emotions built in our 20-year history.

If you take a break from your computer for a few minutes, the screen saver appears. Eventually you return to the computer, tap on the mouse, and the file that you were working on reappears on the screen. The file that appears is only as long or short, meaningful or shallow as what you had written before. When you click on the mouse, you never expect the tap to create the contents of the file. It only calls up whatever already exists.

Walking into a synagogue is like tapping on the mouse. It brings up a file. If you have written an extensive file, then all the emotions connected to that file will be evoked. If you have written only a small file, you can only expect to draw on the little that is already there.

Many of us walk into a synagogue with the expectation that a spiritual experience will descend upon us, regardless of how much or little we have written in our own personal Godfile. We expect that the setting, prayer book, or maybe even the singing, will elicit spiritual feelings. But in truth, neither the synagogue nor the prayerbook can create a spiritual connection.

During the time of formal prayer, it is practically impossible to *create* a relationship with God. The synagogue can only serve to remind you of a relationship that already exists. Praying in a synagogue can certainly eclipse many of life's distractions, and help focus a relationship with God, but it is very unlikely that it will actually create the relationship. When no Godfile has been written, and thus no file appears, frustration and disillusionment set in. The process is not magical. A file in which nothing has been written will produce just that – nothing. It is not the computer's fault. It is not the fault of the synagogue or the prayerbook: they are simply tools designed to help us bring up the Godfile.

Just as in any relationship, it takes effort to build a relationship with God – effort that takes place in many settings besides the synagogue.

Only you can write your own Godfile.

Writing Your Own Godfile

How does one write a Godfile?

For many years I taught students about the history, composition and meaning of the Jewish prayerbook, trying to impart the beauty, depth and wisdom of its words, and the pivotal role it has played in uniting the Jewish people through space and time.

It was frustrating to see so many students absorbing this information about prayer on a purely intellectual level, with little translation into meaningful relationships with God. What had gone wrong? My aim was to instill a desire to intensify our relationship with God through prayer, and I did not want the learning to be a purely academic exercise.

Together with friends and colleagues, I reflected on this dilemma. Is there any point in imparting knowledge if it does not open the gateways to self-knowledge and a spiritual understanding? Can this spiritual impasse be overcome?

We experimented with new ideas, three of which we found to be particularly helpful:
1. Spiritual Retreats and Workshops
2. Spiritual Moments
3. Spiritual Check-ups

1. Spiritual Retreats and Workshops

I have always loved the classroom setting, first as a student and now as a teacher. But the limitations of the classroom have become increasingly clear to me.

My children and I spend a lot of time together. We hang out, play, and sometimes learn together. In the past, I often felt frustrated by what I perceived to be a lack of intimacy and personal focus during our time together. So many hours were spent in each others' company, yet I wondered how much of this time was meaningful or memorable. After a while, I came to the conclusion that part of the problem was that at home we are inevitably distracted by whatever is going on at the moment; people wandering in and out, the phone ringing, housework needing to be done. I found it virtually impossible to give my kids undivided attention at home.

I realized that any time spent outside of our home – regardless of what we would do and where we would go – created a bond impossible to simulate inside the house. The children also felt it. It wasn't that we had to do earth-shattering things together outside of the home. The simple act of leaving the house provided a welcome break from routine expectations and distractions, helping us break free from family roles.

So my children and I established what we called the "exploring team." We would go out without a clear plan, often without any idea where we were going. We would not hesitate to take new paths, to stop and examine new things. We were not afraid of getting lost; each new trail brought new discoveries.

In my teaching career, I adopted this model for some "spiritual exploring" as well. Inside the classroom, my students and I were often stuck in our respective roles, locked into certain expected behavior patterns. We needed to "get out."

So we went on a "spiritual retreat." Several years ago, my

students and I packed our bags and headed to the desert, where nature's quiet serenity and beauty were especially conducive to spiritual exploration.

Structure of the Workshops

During this retreat, we ran spiritual workshops. The aim was to encourage full integration of the ideas into our everyday lives. The workshops stemmed from my personal frustration regarding academic-only methods of teaching and study. Often, despite my understanding and enjoyment of the material, I sensed only partial engagement, and experienced a sense of disconnection. I comprehended everything, yet the material did not alter my life in any way.

Perhaps this problem stemmed from my approach to the ideas studied. I come from a family of scientists, philosophers and doctors. I cannot remember the last time anyone in my family acted spontaneously. During a family reunion, I once joked that if we really want to let our hair down, we play chess. While I have always respected intellectual rigor, I now recognized that it was holding me back. My obsession with intellectual precision had become an obstacle blocking my ability to integrate the learning into my life. I was often "over-thinking," unable to listen to any part of myself other than my mind.

In the workshops, we were able to go beyond our heads and enter into our hearts. The structure of the workshops themselves facilitated the process. They were designed in accordance with the Jewish mystical understanding of the nature of the soul. According to the Kabbalah, inner voices are expressed in three dimensions: the mind, the heart and the body. In Kabbalistic terms, these three spheres of being are called the *Neshama* (intellectual drive), the *Ruach* (emotional drive) and the *Nefesh* (physical drive).

The *Neshama* voice expresses the mind, continuously channeling the content and direction of thinking. It continually elevates and sanctifies my thoughts.

The *Ruach* voice channels the meditations of the "heart," the emotional world. It urges the uplifting of emotions and character traits, impelling deeper relationships built through love, compassion and personal meaning.

The *Nefesh* voice deals with the physical self, including the visible world and natural drives. It urges human beings to elevate and refine their physical drives, and to use them as an expression of meaningful life.

Mind, heart and body. In an ideal educational setting, all three of these elements are accessed and harmonized. Each dimension interacts with the others. No aspect of the individual is ignored or denied.

In light of this understanding of the soul, each of our spiritual workshops contained three components:

1. First we engaged the *Neshama* voice, the mind, through the study of a spiritual idea.
2. Then we engaged the *Ruach* voice through activities designed to connect our hearts to this material. For example we would ask a series of personal trigger questions, a process that we eventually referred to as a "spiritual check-up."
3. Finally, we created programming that helped us engage our *Nefesh* voice. Sometimes we would express our physical selves through creative writing, art, sculpture or movement. The quality of the works of art was irrelevant. Expression on the physical plane gave life and reality to the intangible ideas and emotions.

The setting and structure of these workshops had as profound an effect on me as on the other participants, altering my previous approach to education. The trigger questions forced me to reflect on how I personally related to each subject. The creative writing and/or art workshop encouraged me to express externally what had previously been locked within my mind and heart.

At first, I was uncomfortable with the more experiential aspects of the workshop. I felt self-conscious over the quality of what I created. Was my writing filled with clichés? Did my artwork resemble that of a third-grader? How could I possibly share this with others? What would they think of me? Yet, surprisingly, after a period of time, I actually found myself enjoying the experiential part of the workshops the most. A process of creation and newness was taking place. I would never really know what I was going to produce until it came out of me. Most eye-opening and especially meaningful for me was how powerful a learning process this venue of expression was. It connected me to the material and continually provided me with insights that the pure examination of the material did not.

2. Spiritual Moments

Another valuable tool in writing your Godfile is the sharing of spiritual moments.

It is difficult to feel spiritually connected all the time. Our everyday routine demands much of our attention and energy. But every so often, a spiritual moment will occur in our lives; an intense, meaningful, unforgettable moment that can be recalled, often with vivid detail and emotional clarity. These moments are like treasure boxes which can be opened at any time, even months after the event. They have such beauty that we catch our breath at their potency. And when we remember these moments, they have the power to reconnect us immediately with the awe we felt then.

What constitutes a "spiritual moment?" Spiritual moments are subjective. Each individual decides for him or herself what defines a "spiritual moment." It does not have to occur within a religious context. People do not have to be talking about God or making theological statements. For many, spiritual moments are connected with life-and-death situations; for others, with a dramatic turning point in their lives or a remarkable turn of events. A spiritual moment can be a sudden awareness of the grandeur of nature, or a seemingly "plain" moment that takes place within an everyday setting.

In my teaching career, I love watching and listening to students share their spiritual moments. Inevitably, they are transported back to the sensation and wonder they felt during the original experience, as if they are reliving it all over again. One man described with emotion the night his family left Egypt in secret in 1958. Over forty years later, he remarked with tears in his eyes, "Yes, I see the steps up to the airplane. I can feel my father's hand holding mine."

For many, sharing and listening to spiritual moments in a public setting makes a dramatic impact, helping to affirm a personal spiritual quest. Even people who initially had difficulty recalling a "spiritual moment" began to remember experiences after hearing others share their stories and were eager to share them with the group. The act of sharing takes on a momentum of its own, helping to create a sense of sincerity, candidness, and yearning for spiritual growth.

One student spoke of never having cried after the sudden death of his father. A tough divorce lawyer shared that she had experienced a profound spiritual moment when her 20-year-old daughter asked to cuddle with her. A young woman who had never found spiritual meaning within her work, said that she was now motivated to change professions, and subsequently did.

Life is full of potentially transformative moments. Tapping into the memory of these moments, even if they occurred decades earlier, enables reconnection to the vitality and hope they once evoked, revitalizing one's desire to create new moments of personal and powerful connection.

Given the opportunity to share spiritual moments within a public setting, many individuals feel overwhelmingly grateful, and benefit greatly from the chance to reflect and focus on the spiritual dimension of their lives. Many find renewed hope in a life occupied with self-analysis, critique, and a desperate search to fill voids. After I led a group of rabbis in this practice, one commented that the experience had been more powerful to him than the actual Rosh HaShana prayers. Remarkable.

A Participant's Personal Spiritual Moment:

My parents are Jewish, but my family belonged to a Protestant church. At home, my parents gave everything Jewish a negative spin. If someone did something rude, dumb or unappealing, the reaction was always: Stop acting so Jewish! I always felt out of place no matter where I went, like someone who's been disowned and can't adjust to it.

When I was a junior at Bennington in the late 1980s, I wanted to visit Israel. I don't know what inspired this. I live by my hunches.

Unfortunately, I was out of place in the overseas program at Ben-Gurion University in Beersheba. The other students were American Jews who'd gone through Jewish youth groups and summer camps – booster types who sang all the songs, knew all the vocabulary and didn't seem to have any Jewish identity problems. After a couple of months in the wrong place, I made plans to go home, wondering why my hunch had been wrong.

Because I was already in Israel, I figured I ought to do some obligatory sightseeing. Near the end of my stay, I went to Jerusalem with a non-Jewish friend from Finland who was volunteering in Israel. We went to the Western Wall. Okay, nice stones, but it didn't do anything for me. I'd done my sightseeing and was leaving the Western Wall plaza to go back to Beersheba, back to America, when a stranger struck up a conversation with my friend and me. Were we interested in Judaism? Would we like to join a religiously observant family for Shabbat?

I didn't quite know what Shabbat was. But the stranger seemed nice and talked about opportunities to learn about Judaism. That clicked a switch in my cranky brain. After all, wasn't that why I had come to Israel to begin with? Why not? Let's go for it.

I looked the part. I was wearing a vintage antique dress – long sleeves and skirt. We got sent to a family in Mea Shearim (an extremely religious neighborhood in Jerusalem). They didn't speak any English and we didn't speak any Yiddish, but somehow we communicated. They were giving, sincere people. In their home I felt myself entering a religious experience that seemed real. I didn't understand the rituals, I didn't know the Yiddish table-songs, and I couldn't even chat with them, but all evening I felt something touching me deeply, as if my heart recognized and understood it all.

Later that evening, my friend said goodbye quickly and disappeared, like someone escaping a bad experience. When I found him the next day in Beersheba, he explained his hasty departure. "I've traveled a lot," he said, "and I've swum easily in a lot of different places. But I've never felt so much like a stranger, so completely that I didn't belong, that I was in the wrong place."

I experienced exactly the opposite. I couldn't say why, but I felt I'd finally found my place. My friend's aversion, like a magnet set to the wrong pole of another magnet, made me realize that he was different from me. Simply put, we came from different roots. For a girl like me, brought up in a Presbyterian church, it was a revelation. I was a Jew after all. Maybe that was why, with my confused background, I had always felt out of place. My hunch long ago had been right.

I never saw the Mea Shearim family again. They probably have no idea what effect they had on me, but they opened me up to explore Judaism. I'm still searching. It's been a twisting road, but I know that, having found my home in Judaism, it's impossible for me to be someone else ever again.

3. Spiritual Check-ups

A third valuable tool in writing your Godfile is having a spiritual check-up.

I celebrated my fortieth birthday in Milwaukee. It was Shabbat, and I had been invited to the home of a *hassidic* Rabbi, Rav Michel Twerski, for lunch. I mentioned to him that this was a special day for me, that my fortieth birthday symbolized a rite of passage to a new stage in life. He asked me what I was going to do to mark the event. I replied that many of my friends had been nudging me to go to a doctor to get a physical. Rav Twerski stared at me in silence. After a few minutes, he remarked that he thought it was interesting that my friends had advised me to get a *physical* check-up. "Do you know what I advise people to do when they turn 40? I tell them that they should go and have a '*spiritual* check-up.' Why should we take any less care of the soul than of the body?"

From that point on, the rabbi's words reverberated in my mind, but I did not know how to put them into practice. What would it mean to have a spiritual check-up? When I need a physical check-up, I know exactly what to do and where to go. The body undergoes routine tests and examinations. But how do I arrange a spiritual check-up? Who would give it? What questions would be asked?

I decided to experiment with Rav Twerski's idea.

For my first spiritual check-up, a student and I began by asking each other a question: "How would my life be different if I were more spiritually connected?" For that moment, we placed our theological issues and questions in abeyance. We did not explain or justify our words. We just talked.

"If I were more spiritually connected," I started, "I would worry less. I think that I would be more patient, more compassionate. I would get less caught up in the inevitable, daily, annoying moments. I would also appreciate the small blessings more. I think that I would try to allow my life to flow more, with less of a compulsion to control and order it. Maybe I would even smile more."

I recall thinking at the time that I was not sure where these words were coming from. They were certainly not thought out or planned. Some of my comments seemed banal, even clichéd, but I didn't let that bother me. I tried not to censor my words. I took full advantage of this opportunity to let my thoughts flow naturally and honestly, without worrying about what came out. I spoke from my heart.

Over the past few years, I have shared this experience of "spiritual check-ups" with several thousand people. Students and peers, ranging in age and in religious background were asking themselves for the first time direct questions about spirituality. Many tears were shed during this cathartic experience. An unknown source of emotion had been welling up inside these people for years, waiting to be acknowledged and released. They had experienced their first spiritual check-up, and the process of spiritual healing was underway.

How to Have a Spiritual Check-Up

Like all check-ups, the goal of a spiritual check-up is to assess what needs more attention and should be corrected, and to affirm what is working well and should be continued. Unlike regular check-ups, however, there are no right or wrong answers in a spiritual check-up. And there is no doctor; each person gives him or herself the check-up.

There are two essential components to a spiritual check-up:

1. A listening partner, and
2. A safe space environment

Listening Partner

The key to a successful physical check-up is having a good doctor. The key to a successful spiritual check-up is having a good partner, one who focuses entirely on listening to the other. The partner must be an active, compassionate listener, whose only goal is to listen and understand without judgment or confrontation.

For years I could not understand why it was that certain people had the ability to bring out a deeper, more articulate, part of me. What were these people doing? Why did I always sense this change in myself in their presence? Then I realized that these people weren't just *hearing* the words coming out of my mouth. They were *deeply* listening, *totally focused* on what I had to say. Their deep listening would trigger my own ability to listen deeply to myself, helping me give expression to profound and hidden thoughts.

During the spiritual check-up, partners take turns asking each other questions. There is no rush; it takes time for deep, previously constrained thoughts to emerge. Periods of silence are often essential to allow the next wave of reflection to surface. Profound answers reside deep within, and patience and effort may be required to bring them to the surface.

Though it might sound excessive, forty minutes has proven to be the ideal amount of time to devote to a spiritual check-up. Fifteen minutes should be allocated for each person's initial response to the questions, followed by another five minutes for each partner to express further thoughts kindled by the process. If forty minutes is not possible, however, even 20 minutes can be beneficial.

Safe Space Environment

The check-up must take place in an environment of "safe space." Without a supportive environment, one's mind may be present, but the heart will be absent. New territory cannot be freely explored if a person feels anxious or fears confrontation. Since transformation involves taking risks, an encouraging, empathetic environment is required to allow people to show their vulnerability.

The physical location is unimportant. A busy parking lot can be just as effective as an isolated beach at sunset. The more peaceful and beautiful the setting, the easier it is to trigger self-exploration, but the most crucial factor is the willingness of each partner to create a "safe space," withholding judgment and evaluation.

Do not attempt to provide concrete solutions to your partner's problems. The goal is to help each other achieve greater self-awareness and clarity, not to steer him or her toward a particular way of thinking or direction in life. Refrain from giving advice. Only reflective questions, such as "How long have you felt this way?" or "How does this make you feel?" should be asked. Leading, practical questions like "Have you ever considered doing _____?" or "Why don't you _____?" reflect the approach of the person asking the question rather than the one undergoing self-exploration.

Personal growth cannot be achieved in a setting that lacks mutual trust, support, openness and empathy. I was once teaching a class on prayer. We were sitting in a circle, and the discussion became quite personal and intense. At one point, after one student shared a personal insight, another rolled her eyes. It only took a split second; she might not even have been aware of the action. Immediately, though, the atmosphere in the class shifted; everyone closed down and disconnected. No one dared risk becoming the next target of "rolling eyes." I immediately recognized how different the atmosphere would have been in a circle of unreserved compassion.

A spiritual check-up may also be conducted as a preparation for prayer services. Discussing the questions below before the start of a regular service can transform the prayer experience. In addition, any quiet time during the week may be conducive for a spiritual check-up. Below are some examples of questions that can be asked during a spiritual check-up:

Spiritual Check-Up Questions

1. How would I characterize my relationship with God?
2. How would my life be different if I had a closer relationship with God?
3. What is holding me back from having a closer relationship with God?

4. What is one practical thing I could do that would help develop a closer relationship with God?

5. Who is my spiritual role model? What is it about this person that I wish to emulate?

Now that we have looked at these three ideas – spiritual retreats, sharing spiritual moments and spiritual check-ups – we can ask ourselves again: How does one write a Godfile? How does one deepen a spiritual connection?

If we want to build and maintain a relationship with God, we need to invest in it (through spiritual retreats), cherish it (through spiritual moments), and nourish it (through spiritual check-ups). These tools are invaluable for supporting us through the process. Just as in our relationships with spouses, family and friends, we cannot expect an instant connection with God. A solid foundation must be built before bonds can be formed. We need to engage our whole beings in the process – our minds, hearts and bodies. Once we have applied ourselves to this goal, we are well on our way to writing our own personal Godfile.

Overcoming Obstacles to Writing Your Godfile

We may find that in our path to writing a Godfile, we encounter obstacles along the way, both internal and external.

Internal Obstacle #1: The Spiritual Stereotype

One common obstacle is the pervasive stereotype of the "spiritual type." Often I ask groups of students, "What do spiritual people do? What do they look like? What do spiritual people eat?" I inevitably receive the same answers: "They are mellow," says one. "They meditate a lot," says another. Others will say, "They do yoga, they sing, they dance, they are probably vegetarian or vegan, they wear flowing clothes, probably white." Then I ask the group, "How many of you fit into these categories?" Rarely does a hand go up.

"What is the goal of becoming more spiritual?" I persist. Again, the answers usually include such stereotypical notions as, "being at peace with oneself, achieving nirvana, calmness and serenity. An inner glow."

Unfortunately, this characterization is terribly limiting. And since most people do not match this limited image, they believe that they themselves lack spirituality. These preconceived notions discourage most from ever trying to pursue a more spiritual path. I cannot begin to count the number of people who have told me, "I am simply not a spiritual person. I am not the spiritual type."

Overcoming the Obstacle: Breaking the Stereotype

I often ask people if they think they have a soul. They almost always respond affirmatively. "Well," I continue, "what does this soul do? What does it occupy itself with? Does it 'just sit there,' or is it active in any manner? Have you ever felt your soul communicating something to you? Have you ever had a spiritual moment?"

Invariably, one person begins to open up, and others begin to nod in agreement.

At the closing circle of one of our retreats, we invited everyone to talk for a few minutes about where they were spiritually. One elderly man had barely opened his mouth during our three days together. We hadn't expected him to say anything, so we were surprised when he began to talk and continued for over 20 minutes. Suddenly he stopped talking, and began to shake and cry. With tears welling up in his eyes, he whispered that all of his life he felt he had been on the outside of Judaism looking in. Now, for the first time, he felt as if someone had opened a door to let him in.

Who had locked this man out? Who created this "inside" and "outside" perception? Unfortunately, most of the time we do it to ourselves.

With an unrealistic stereotype of the "spiritual person" firmly embedded in our minds, we close the door to spirituality and lock ourselves out. The essential step in overcoming this obstacle, and placing ourselves back inside, is telling oneself, "I have a soul. I am a spiritual person."

Internal Obstacle #2: Fear of Change

Countering the desire within each of us for growth is an equally strong voice saying, "You're okay as you are, don't mess up your life. Who knows where change will lead? Why bother?"

According to the Talmud, we were all created with a drive that tricks us into complacency. We have a subconscious drive that urges us to remain static, to resist growth.

Sometimes when we see people after a long absence we observe that they haven't changed. Are they stable? Or are they stuck? One of the most difficult moments for students who return home after a year in Israel occurs when a relative or friend looks disapprovingly at them and remarks, "You've changed," subtly implying that change is a negative development reflecting a lack of stability.

At various stages in my life, an internal voice urged me to resist any kind of change. I convinced myself that more than anything, I needed to regain a sense of stability. I would often worry and feel uncertain about what a possible new stage might demand of me. Sometimes I simply lacked the energy and emotional strength to consider change and self-growth. For many years, I was aware that I had reached an impasse, and that I was spiritually stuck, yet I found myself incapable of overcoming this block. I was trapped in the daily routine of going through the motions.

Overcoming the Obstacle: Finding the Will to Change

There is no single way to overcome this obstacle. Each person has his or her own personal demons. Personally, my desire to grow finally outweighed my drive to resist change. A spiritual block is like a black cloud that depletes joy and passion.

The crucial step in overcoming this obstacle requires asking ourselves three questions:

- Am I stuck?
- What exactly am I afraid of?
- What is holding me back?

External Obstacle #1:
The Synagogue – Where Is My Voice?

Did you ever feel like walking out of your synagogue?

Why is it that attending synagogue can be such a frustrating, and often empty, experience? Did you ever feel that it just was not working for you? You look around; everyone else is uttering the words, going through the motions. But the words of the prayer book are not your words; the pace of the service is not your pace. You're feeling lonely, alienated, out of it, and the feeling intensifies with each passing moment. Maybe you're wondering, "Am I the only one who feels like this? What's the matter with me?"

Perhaps you are asking yourself, "What am I supposed to be feeling at this moment? What is supposed to be happening now? Should I be asking for something? Should I be crying? Am I supposed to be feeling spiritual? Am I hoping for a mystical breakthrough? I know how to recite the words of the prayerbook, but then what? What am I doing here? Where is my personal voice in all of this? There's no time or room for me to discover how I really feel about all of this. And, most painfully and poignantly of all, what is my voice supposed to be?"

At certain points in my life, the daily routine of praying in synagogue helped me build the stability of my faith. I enjoyed the connection with my friends in synagogue, the camaraderie before and after *davenning* (prayer) and the singing. But did the actual moment of prayer have any impact on my life? Was it meaningful?

I came to realize that for me – then – the answer was no.

Not only did my prayers lack meaning, but they often left me feeling deeply dissatisfied and frustrated, regardless of how many different synagogues I attended.

Overcoming the Obstacle: Finding Your Own Voice

Serious prayer should involve more than just the recitation of liturgical, or even informal, words. Prayer should be an authentically personal experience. It is not *someone's* prayer; it is *your* prayer. The Talmud refers to prayer as "the work of the heart." Prayer should reach the depths of your being and touch your heart.

The prayer book is supposed to be the springboard for this "work of the heart." Sometimes, however, the words of the prayerbook take over, usurping your personal meditations. You follow the lines of the prayer book without personalizing them, without adding words or thoughts. You are not transformed. In fact, there is no "you" there.

You need to somehow find a place for yourself in the prayerbook, to insert your own words, emotions and needs that you are feeling precisely at that moment. You need to bring yourself into the prayer experience.

Is this possible? Can you find room for yourself in the midst of an organized prayer service and fixed liturgy? Human beings are forever changing, but the prayerbook does not: If the prayerbook does not change, how can your own personal experience of prayer evolve to reflect your needs?

The rabbis themselves stressed the need to add personal prayers during the *Amida*, the silent standing prayer. During the "Listen to our voice" (*Shema Koleinu*) section of the *Amida*, one is encouraged to add personal thoughts. At the end of the *Amida*, and even during each blessing of the *Amida*, the rabbis encouraged the inclusion of personal insertions.

The essential step in overcoming this obstacle is saying to

yourself, "I have a voice. I am allowed to add my personal prayers to the words of the prayerbook. What personal words do I want to include?"

External Obstacle #2 –
Public Nature of Prayer in Places of Worship

A second obstacle in creating one's own Godfile is the focus of religious education on the "externals" of prayer, often at the expense of the "internals." Instead of concentrating on developing a rich internal life, and tapping into our spiritual beings, there has been a preoccupation with mastering the mechanics and technique of prayer.

I recognized this phenomenon while working with my students. They were talented young adults from all over the world. For many of them, this was their first serious encounter with Judaism. They began to learn about Jewish ideas and gradually incorporated more religious observances into their lives. They inevitably began to think about joining a Jewish community and wondered how they would fit in. How would they manage socially in this new milieu? Would it be awkward? Would they stand out? Would they feel self-conscious?

In their desire to integrate into Jewish communities, they pushed themselves to learn the essentials of Jewish public life: how to say the prayers, when to stand and when to bow. Some even learned how to lead the prayers. These were the easy things to teach and to learn.

Because of the public nature of places of worship, students became consumed with learning about the more visible and social dimensions of prayer. They often avoided the deeper question of how to use prayer to express their relationship with God.

Overcoming the Obstacle:
Finding Your Private Space in Places of Worship

Prayer comes in a number of forms. Certain forms center on the individual experience, a solitary figure sitting in solitude, in meditation, in supreme aloneness.

In community-centered prayer, the individual is swallowed up in the group experience. I remember being spellbound watching a Christian "revival" that culminated in a community singing of Halleluyah. In the frenetic energy of the congregation, the individuals seemed to merge into one communal being.

Which of these paradigms of prayer most reflects Judaism's approach – a solitary experience or a communal one? Actually, neither. Rather, the moment of encountering God in Jewish prayer reflects the fusion of these two models.

Although the *Shema* is probably the most well-known Jewish prayer, the central and most important moment in Jewish prayer is the silent standing prayer, the *Amida*. The *Shema* always precedes the *Amida*.

At the beginning of the *Amida*, one takes three steps backward, followed by three steps forward. Although one is now standing physically in the same spot, on a spiritual level, one moves into an entirely different place when entering the "*Amida* space." Despite being surrounded by others, the person praying is in a very private space – a space which draws upon the spiritual energy and mood of those around us, but that leaves us utterly alone at the ultimate moment of prayer. Students often refer to it as "the encounter" or "the zone" of standing in the presence of God.

Unfortunately, the social and communal nature of the synagogue and prayer often eclipse this precious moment. Extra effort is necessary to regain this sense and sanctity of private, solitary space. The rabbis of the Talmud instruct that one should not take any notice of any interruption – not even the entry of a king into the room or the sensing of a snake wrapped around one's legs. At this moment of silent prayer, one is entering a spiritual twilight zone, and nothing else exists but our relationship with God.

Three steps backward, three steps forward. You are alone with yourself. What are you thinking?

Once you enter your "three steps forward" space, you enter sacred space, beyond time. You may find it helpful to pause, take several deep breaths, and repeat to yourself: "Three steps backward, three steps forward. I just entered into a different zone of being."

The rest of the congregation may be rushing forward with their own prayers, but you can and should take as long as you want during your private silent prayer. This is your time with God and everything else will simply have to wait.

After having taken three steps backward and three steps forward, what is supposed to happen now?

This moment cannot be captured through the words of the Jewish prayerbook. It may be beyond all words. It is your opportunity to connect to the deepest part within yourself, to something greater than yourself. This is an experience that cannot be dictated for you by others, a moment of self-definition that only you can create for yourself. Only you will ever know what has transpired during this interval. Will this moment be meaningful? Or will it be empty?

Three steps backward, three steps forward. What kind of space have you entered? That depends on how you prepared yourself for this moment. The community cannot be held responsible for the depth, or lack of depth, of this spiritual moment. You have total control over the quality of the private space that you create during prayer.

The important step in overcoming this obstacle is asking yourself, "Have I entered into a sacred space? What has changed within me? What does this open up within me?"

Bringing the Godfile into Life

There were times during synagogue prayer when I would sense two separate realities: a "regular life reality" and a "synagogue reality." I noticed that the minute people started to pray, their behavior changed. I sensed falseness. It seemed to me that I was a spectator observing a pious charade, a script of religious role playing.

I did not want to assume another identity once I started to pray. I did not want my prayer to be a cloak that I could put on and then take off as soon as I had finished uttering the last words of the prayer. I did not want prayer to be a moment disconnected from my entire life. Rather, I hoped that prayer would be a natural act that would inform and enhance my whole life. Serious prayer does not solely focus on a relationship between myself and the Infinite, it also impacts on how I relate to other people. Since human beings are created in the image of God, the way that I relate to God parallels and influences the way that I relate to each individual.

Everything that is true like this ↑↓ (vertical, symbolizing relationships with God) is also true like this ⇄ (horizontal, symbolizing relationships with other people).

Throughout life, we cultivate relationships with our parents, friends and loved ones. In the same vein, we cultivate a relationship with God during prayer. The only difference is that prayer creates a connection with a force that we cannot see. Each relationship that is developed influences all our other relationships. If I am in love, all of my other relationships begin to take on a new glow. Likewise, if I am furious at someone, then this anger will inevitably spill over onto all those surrounding me. No relationship can be viewed in isolation; everything is connected. It thus stands to reason that whatever kind of relationship I cultivate and develop with God during prayer will also affect all of my interpersonal relationships.

One complaint I often hear is, "Why is it so important to get in touch with my spiritual side? Why isn't it enough to be a good person, to live like a *mensch* (an upright individual)?" This is indeed an extremely valid complaint when the spiritual side of a person is not influencing his or her behavior.

But that is not how it is supposed to be. When there is no connection between a person's inner and outer life, the result is that this individual is not leading a whole and integrated life, but is acting out a pious charade.

The true test of spirituality is how one brings God into all relationships. As a result of prayer, are you a more patient, more loving and more compassionate spouse? Are you a better child, parent, friend?

To help integrate the "inner" and "outer" dimensions of life, each chapter in Part 11 will include a section entitled: "Bringing the Godfile into my life."

Everything that is true like this ⇅ is also true like this ⇌.

PART II

Clicking Up
the Godfile

Clicking Up the Godfile

The Godfile is written during the course of a lifetime. But how can you make sure that yours is kept up to date? As with all relationships, your relationship with God can become stale if it is only being maintained by earlier conversations and bonding. How can you keep it alive and vital?

Prayer, whether daily, weekly, or even monthly, is supposed to be the "check-in" time in one's ongoing relationship with God. It is similar to the phone call home in the middle of the day. A relationship with God cannot be *created* during prayer; rather, it reminds the prayer of the relationship, allowing a brief refocus on the spiritual life. Click on the mouse of life; bring up the Godfile.

There are times in life which inspire each and every person to pray. When I was a soldier in the Israeli army, I was the only one in my unit who would pray regularly. Although some of the men respected this, others expressed skepticism. But once, during a particularly difficult incident, all of my fellow soldiers turned to me as if on cue and said, "Aryeh, don't fight now, we want you to pray. Go pray for all of us!"

Although the desire to pray during moments of stress is sincere and understandable, it does not reflect a fully mature relationship with God. Prayer during times of personal difficulty can be compared to a phone call made by a long-lost relative who suddenly needs help: it is a self-serving relationship.

How can we achieve and maintain a mature relationship with God through prayer?

Since people are complex beings, adopting only one approach to prayer can be extremely limiting. In reality, there are a countless number of ways to relate to God. The following pages present ten approaches to prayer, ten different paradigms for reconnecting with the Infinite.

These ten approaches are based on the writings of great thinkers, rabbis and personalities of the past 200 years. Each approach reflects a profound pathway to God. Each possesses a different aspect of truth. To help personalize these approaches, each paradigm is associated with a different personality type.

Consider the ten approaches presented here as tools that can help make the process of prayer a little less frustrating and a little more rewarding. I have personally tried each approach and believe that each one in its own right, is valuable in finding a pathway to God. I strongly encourage you to try out each one for a week or more, even those that initially fail to strike a chord within you.

The rabbis refer to prayer as work, the "work of one's heart." If you begin to regard prayer as the "work of your heart" rather than just as work, you will have the potential to transform prayer, which may have once been tiring and cumbersome, into a personally rewarding experience.

In any case, the benefits of experimenting with these ten pathways can endure beyond any individual prayer session, since each approach epitomizes a whole outlook on life. These approaches not only provide a means of enhancing one's prayer, they also guide us toward living a life that is connected to God.

The Judge

[The Hebrew infinitive] *"L'hitpallel"* (to pray), from which *"tefillah"* (prayer) is derived, originally meant to deliver an opinion about oneself, **to judge oneself...** Thus it denotes **to step out of active life in order to attempt to gain a true judgment about oneself,** that is, about one's ego, about one's relationship to God and the world... It strives to infuse the mind and heart with the power of such judgment that will direct both renewed to a life of action – purified, sublimated, strengthened. The procedure of arousing such self-judgment is called *"tefillah."*

Rabbi Samson Raphael Hirsch *

---

* Rabbi Samson Raphael Hirsch, *Horev, a Philosophy of Jewish Laws and Observances,*

Three steps backward, three steps forward. You are alone with yourself. What are you thinking?

According to Rabbi Samson Raphael Hirsch, the Hebrew verb *"L'hitpallel,"* which we now translate to mean, "to pray," once meant to deliver an opinion about oneself, to judge oneself.

When you "pray," it is the ideal time to evaluate life, to re-visit today, the past week, the last month… maybe even your entire life. In the silence of this moment, you judge yourself.

At this moment, you are not being emotional, you are not being mystical. You are not reflecting on the problems of other people or of the world. You are thinking about your own life, using all of your rational, cognitive abilities to judge yourself. You are on trial. All at once, you are the judge, the witness and the accused.

The judgment begins. What is the goal of this moment of judgment?

You should hope (pray) for a transformation, a new you. Self-judgment is not reserved exclusively for Yom Kippur. By the time you are ready to conclude this moment of prayer, you should have come to some new resolution about your life, even if only a small one. You are not looking for a moment of epiphany or clarity. You are not waiting for a spiritual lightning bolt to give you a sign.

You are focusing your attention on the tiny creases, the minuscule wrinkles of your life, that you want to straighten out. Each time you enter this zone of silence, you must ask yourself: "Was I patient with my kids this morning? Did I listen to their questions? Did I take an extra moment to seek out the questions they may have wanted to ask, but could

trans. Dayan Dr. I. Grunfeld, Soncino Press, New York, 1981, p. 472.

not find a voice to do so? Did I speak kindly with my partner? Was I careful driving to work? Did I greet people with a smile? Am I doing all that I can to be a good person? Am I doing enough?" The answer is inevitably, "No." It has to be. No person has completely fulfilled his or her potential. Have you ever lived a week, a day, or even an hour, exactly as you could or should have? You are not necessarily trying to achieve a radical transformation, though one is always welcome – and possible. A small one will do.

Why seek this change now? Why in a moment of prayer? Because in the midst of your everyday life, you are simply too busy living to stop and reflect. You race from family to work, from one concern to another. It seems as if there is barely time to catch one's breath in this daily marathon. Yet if you do *not* stop, you run the risk of losing control of yourself and of your life. You probably often ask yourself whether you are controlling your life, or whether life is controlling you. You need to find the time to check in, to make sure that your life is on track, to ensure that you are not rushing too fast or in the wrong direction.

Three steps backward, three steps forward.

Prayer is your time to take a thorough look at yourself. Prayer offers a few moments each and every day to reflect. It provides a chance to stop and revisit the day's events.

You resolve to focus your attention on a single matter. You form a concrete plan of action. Perhaps you plan to do something special with that child who needs attention, or you decide to focus more on a particular student or friend. Maybe you will return your parent's call or will return a book that you borrowed from your neighbor a month ago, but forgot to give back. A concrete resolution, a mini-transformation: that is all you are looking for. You conclude your prayer with three steps backward and return to the hustle of life.

Many students have shared that they have found this approach to prayer to be the most accessible. They are in control of their thoughts and they are not being asked to do anything that is out of character for them. Praying in this way is primarily an intellectual, not an emotional or spiritual, process. However, they also revealed that this approach can also be extremely painful. It is as if you are experiencing a mini-Yom Kippur.

A student once approached me on the last day of classes. We had learned together for a whole year, three times a week, for four hours at a stretch. Out of all of my students, she was the one whom I feared had not gotten much out of the class. She came to me and said, "I know that you might think that I have not changed much this year. But," she said, holding up two fingers a tiny distance apart, "I've changed *this* much. And for me," she continued, "*this* was equivalent to moving a mountain." Sometimes even the smallest change can require the greatest effort.

When you adopt this approach to prayer, you are standing in judgment of yourself. You are asking yourself tough questions. Are you paying attention to how you are living your life? Are you too complacent? Have your self-expectations dwindled? Are you too content with your status quo? You may be aware on a cognitive level that you need to change, but change does not occur by itself. If even the slightest change is to take place, you have to focus your thoughts on solving the problem and creating a plan of action.

We have established that this approach provides a time and place for asking yourself those crucial questions, but you may wonder what this approach to prayer has to do with God. Can self-evaluation really constitute prayer? How does this approach affect your relationship with God, or God's relationship with you? Isn't this just another form of therapy?

It is true that in this approach to prayer, the primary focus is the individual, not God. After all, you are essentially judging yourself. Yet all relationships are interwoven. Once you actively demonstrate the will and desire to change your behavior, then you are no longer the same person that you once were. You have transformed yourself. This self-transformation may in turn act as a catalyst in the way that God relates to you. Rabbi Yosef Albo said: "If one changes his being, then one's fate is also redetermined" (*Sefer HaIkkarim*).

Summary:

This approach to prayer invites you to take a break from the demands and pressure of everyday life. To take a moment for self-reflection, for self-judgment. Praying in this way allows you to revisit and evaluate your life so that you can resolve to make a concrete, albeit small, transformation. This change may, in turn, have a ripple effect and influence God's response to you.

Bringing the Godfile into your life:

As you learn to evaluate yourself through the eyes of God during your moment of prayer, you will also find yourself able to apply this approach to the other relationships in your life, and to evaluate yourself through the eyes of friends and peers. Are you providing your friends or family what they need? How are your actions affecting them? What could you do that would help to improve their lives? What happens if you change some mode of your behavior, in even the smallest way? What happens in a relationship when one partner changes his or her patterns of behavior?

I used to experience difficulty in relating to one particular member of my family. Every time we talked, we would inevitably get into the same argument that we had had dozens of times before. I could see the outcome of the "conversation" an hour before it had finished. But what would happen, I asked myself, if all of a sudden, I chose not to respond in the same predictable fashion? The next time we met up, I tried deviating from the expected script. Instead of engaging in the argument, I just said, "It is great to see you again." He was stymied. He could not respond in his usual way. The mold had been broken. It was as if he was dealing with a new person. The old "me" that was so familiar to him was gone. Now, he also had to respond in a new way. The change in my behavior caused us to relate to each other in a new and more positive way.

Regarding prayer, R. Albo wrote, "When a person changes the level that he is on, or attempts to change the level that he is on, then the heavenly decree changes accordingly."

The same reasoning can be applied to human relationships: when you change the way you relate to someone, even on the smallest level, you can expect to notice a change in his or her response to you.

Everything that is true like this ⇅ *is also true like this* ⇌.

The Judge – A Spiritual Check-Up

1. If I could live this day over, the three things that I would change are:
   A. _____
   B. _____
   C. _____

2. If I had to improve one area of my life, it would be _____.

3. If I had to choose one relationship that needed more attention, it would be _____.

4. The one person that I judge too harshly, and need to show more empathy toward, is _____.

5. The one person who would benefit from my judging his or her behavior is _____.

The Lover

There is a good way which is suitable for all and "very close" indeed – *to arouse and kindle the light of the love that is implanted and concealed in one's heart* so that it may shine forth with its intense light, like a burning fire, in the consciousness of the heart and mind. This [way] is to take to heart the meaning of the verse: "As in water, face to face, so is the heart of man to man" (Proverbs 27:19). The same identical face which a person presents to the water is reflected back to him from the water. So indeed the love of a person for another is reflected back to him. For this love awakens a loving response in the heart of another, cementing their mutual

love and loyalty for each other, especially as each sees
his friend's love for him.

Rabbi Shneur Zalman of Liadi *

*Three steps backward, three steps forward. You are alone with
yourself. What are you thinking?*

"…To arouse and kindle the light of the love that is implanted
and concealed in my heart."

During this time of prayer, you are not asking for anything.
You are not judging yourself. You are not being analytical or
thoughtful. This is not a prayer of the mind. You are trying
to open your heart and express your love for God.

Why? Because you realize that God loves you. The very fact
that you are alive, that you woke up this morning, shows that
God has returned your soul to you for another day. You did
not create yourself. You did not create your body or give yourself a soul. Even the thoughts and qualities that are uniquely
yours are gifts that you have received. Even on the bleakest
day, when you cannot see anything special about yourself,
God returns your soul to you. This is God's act of love, and
acts of love evoke responses of love. "As in water, face to face,
so is the heart of man to man." Like a reflection in the water,
when I receive love, I respond with love.

This is a prayer of giving. You are no longer the focus of
your life. You are not thinking about what you need or what
you would like to receive. You want to take this opportunity
to express gratitude for your life. At this moment in time, you
are not riddled with existential angst. You are not perplexed by
questions like: "Why do the righteous suffer and the wicked

---

* Rabbi Shneur Zalman of Liadi, *Likutei Amarim, Tanya,* Kehot Publication Society,
London, 1981, chapter 46, p. 241.

prosper?" You do not even dwell on such questions as: "What is my purpose in life?" or: "Who am I really?" Your life and the lives of those around you may be lacking in many areas, but you do not focus on what is missing at this moment. Now you are letting go of the many frustrations and disappointments in life that may have embittered you. You have only one thought on your mind: you did not create yourself. You did not ask for your life, nor bring yourself into being. It was all a gift. You may not know why you were created. You may not be sure what your special gifts are, or what you have to offer the world, but those questions can wait. Right now, you are simply thankful for your life. As simple as that.

Can love be aroused through such an approach? When I asked my students to attempt to practice this approach, they experienced great difficulty. They laughed nervously and made jokes. "Do I look like a love machine?" one asked. "I cannot just turn on a switch and become loving, or let my defenses down so quickly," said another. "It is hard to open my heart, hard to get into the zone. Maybe we should open a bottle of wine," suggested a third.

To help overcome these obstacles, I have discussed different levels of love with my students. We discussed the lowest form of love, a common though immoral form, whereby you love someone because you want something in return. The students immediately recognized that this type of love is a form of manipulation, using love for personal gain. This is not a love of giving, but rather an exploitative form of taking. The students then mentioned another form of love: loving another so as to receive love in return. While this is still not a complete form of giving, and the love in this case acts as a means to an end, at least the dynamic stays within the realm of loving.

Then a student raised the possibility of loving someone without any hope of receiving something in return, an act of selfless giving. You care about someone else so much that your own needs are secondary. Your primary goal is to give to the person you love. There is no greater way to express one's love.

A student of mine in his forties, who had never been married, once remarked that he would be overjoyed to feel such love, but that he had never experienced it. He had never been in love. Surprised, I asked him: "You have never been in love with anyone? No one at all?" "Nope," he replied, "I guess that I have just never met the right woman." I suggested that perhaps this had less to do with other people, and more to do with his own capacity, or incapacity, to love. For some reason, he was either not ready or not able to give love. He was not open to loving.

Do some people possess greater capacities for love than others?

I once asked my students to close their eyes and think of the one person in the world who most embodies this quality of selfless love. "Who is the most loving person you know? Can you conjure up an image?" Almost immediately, the atmosphere in the room had changed. Students were sitting peacefully, eyes closed, with a serene expression on their smiling faces. After waiting a few minutes, I asked them if they were able to visualize someone who fit this description. They all responded in the affirmative. Then I asked them if they, personally, would want to be more like this person they envisioned. They nodded. One student said, "Yes, I would really love it if someone would have thought of me while doing this exercise." What enables a person to be so loving?

In his prayer, the Lover strives to become this person, to fulfill the ideal of unselfish loving.

Each person has love in his or her heart, but sometimes it requires work to arouse this emotion. There may be something that is blocking a person from demonstrating or actualizing the love he or she has inside. There is no limit to how loving a person can be. Even if you consider yourself to be a deeply loving person, there is always room for exploration and self-growth. You can always strive to reach new levels. The goal is to open up your heart, and only *you* are capable of doing that.

But this approach is not limited to simply *trying* to become a more loving person. The focus must be on *expressing* the love which is latent in the heart. This is a moment of affirmation. It is not enough to understand and acknowledge the love, but keep it buried inside your heart. During moments of intense prayer, love must be articulated. The verbal expression of love further deepens and intensifies its presence.

The essence of this approach – becoming more aware of our capacity to love, and then expressing it aloud – "is a good way which is suitable for all." This approach does not depend upon one's intellect, memory or experience. This approach is "very close" to all. It lies within one's heart.

Summary:

This approach to prayer invites you to discover and express the love that you are capable of giving. It provides you with an opportunity to focus on the love that God bestows upon everyone, and, like a face looking into water, this should naturally evoke a similar response of love from within.

Bringing the Godfile into your life:

As you learn to tap into the source of love inside you, and express love and gratitude to God, the wellspring of love within you will slowly reveal itself and will spill over onto all of your relationships.

When I am teaching a class of young adult students, it is often obvious who is in love. They exude a certain glow as they make their way into the classroom. This radiance, in turn, impacts everyone in the class. They treat others with more patience and kindness. They are less likely to become upset over small things. Sentences like, "Don't worry about it," and "I do not mind," are often heard from such people. When people feel love, they become more expansive, they have more love to give to others.

Essential to this approach is envisioning yourself as a more loving person. Once you become a more loving person, then this loving state of mind will permeate all of your actions. This does not mean that you should ignore the issues or conflicts endemic to every relationship. Every relationship endures periods of turbulence, misunderstandings and disappointments. While you are going through this difficult time in your relationship, however, you can still try to express love to your partner, family member or friend.

Just as you verbally express your feelings of love in the context of prayer, you should also articulate to your spouse, friend or family member the love you have in your heart. The Lover's approach is conducive for articulation of these feelings. Articulating your love in this way will have a positive effect both on you and the person who is the recipient of the love, the lover and the beloved. People are often quick to verbalize what is going wrong in a relationship, but are slow to focus on its positive elements. Affirming the relationship, through ongoing verbal expressions of love and caring, will remind you of the broader context of your relationship, and will prevent "the bad stuff" from obscuring its positive aspects.

What is the result of tapping into your deep capacity to love and then conveying this love to others? A natural spiral of love ensues. The more love that you display to others, the more they will display to you. "So indeed the love of a person for another is reflected back."

Everything that is true like this ↑↓ *is also true like this* ⇄.

The Lover – A Spiritual Check-Up

1. The most loving person I know is _____. The one person who has expressed the most unconditional love *for me* is _____.

2. The most loving, giving moment that I have ever witnessed was _____.

3. If I were a more loving person, my life would be different because _____.

4. The one thing that is holding me back from becoming more loving is _____.

5. The person to whom I need to say "I love you" is _____.

The Listener

Prayer is most true when it expresses the idea that *the soul is continually praying*... At the moment of actual prayer, *the perpetual prayer of the soul is revealed*... Prayer beseeches the soul to convey to her its role... All of one's efforts to learn Torah and acquire wisdom is in order to enable the concealed prayer of the soul to be revealed... When many days or years have passed without serious prayer, toxic stones gather around one's heart and one feels, because of them, a certain heaviness of spirit. When one's "good" spirit returns, and the gift of prayer is bequeathed from the heavens, the obstacles are gradually removed, the many dams that have blocked the free-flowing of the stream of one's soul gradually disappear... This will not occur in one moment, but gradually the splendor of prayer reveals its light.

Rabbi Avraham Yitzhak HaCohen Kook[*]

Three steps backward, three steps forward. You are alone with yourself. What are you thinking?

"The soul is continually praying."

Prayer is not a band-aid or a cure for problems. In this approach to prayer, you are not asking God to solve your problems. You are not looking to satisfy a momentary need, but rather you are seeking the "perpetual prayer of the soul."

The soul is continually praying. It continually attempts to communicate.

The human consciousness is like a radio that has many stations, each one continually broadcasting. When tuned into one station, all of the others continue to broadcast. Occasionally the dial is changed to a different station. Each station broadcasts a different voice: the voice of parents, the voice of friends, and the voice of colleagues. There is a voice pushing for popularity, and there is a voice driving for success. There is a voice advertising fun and enjoyment, and there is a voice speaking of meaning and fulfillment.

All of these voices, these stations, are broadcasting at the same time. You choose which one, or ones, to listen to.

And then there is the station of the soul. The soul, too, is always broadcasting. It is always talking, attempting to get through and make a connection. Twenty-four hours a day, whether listened to or not, the soul, the life-force, is talking.

What is its message? What does it say?

---

[*] Rabbi Avraham Yitzhak HaCohen Kook, *Olat HaRa'aya*, Mossad HaRav Kook, Jerusalem, Israel, 1963, p. 11 (author's translation).

From the onset of my adult life, the following questions have absorbed me, sometimes plagued me, and will never leave me. I address them to God:

"Dear God, I did not choose to be born. I did not choose to be born into this body, this family, or in this time and place. You, in Your infinite wisdom, brought me into this world. Why? What am I supposed to do? What is *my* unique message? What is my mission? Dear God, all I want in this world is to be myself. Who am I really?"

Even after all of my needs are satisfied, these questions continue to lurk in the inner chambers of my being. How do I begin to answer them? Perhaps I have just been wantonly abandoned in this world. Perhaps I will forever be asking myself these questions without ever finding the answers. How will I ever know? Am I just hopelessly lost?

Rav Kook writes that there is a way of knowing; there is the path of personal insight. It is neither complicated nor sophisticated. I may never understand quantum physics. I may never understand why the world functions as it does. But there is a way for me to understand who I am. Each person has a unique contribution to offer the world. How will I discover mine?

How? By just listening.

Your soul is perpetually praying. What is it saying? It is saying, "This is you, this is who you really are, this is your special gift. This is what your contribution to the world could be, should be. This is your message and your mission. Just listen and you will hear it. Listen – and go do it."

The message is not articulated in words or sentences. It is conveyed as a sense, an intuition. Sometimes it will come in the flash of a moment, like a spiritual lightning bolt. Rav Kook writes: "Each time the heart feels a truly spiritual stirring, each time a new and noble thought is born, it is as if an angel of God is knocking, pressing on the doors of the soul, asking that we open our door to him." In effect, there are always "angels knocking on our door."

Did you ever suddenly come to the realization that there was something you just had to do? A moment of clarity that came seemingly, out of nowhere. That may have been the voice of the soul, conveying its message ever so subtly.

Sometimes I have the sense – inexplicably – that I am in the right place at the right time. I have a mysterious feeling that what I am doing at this very moment is what I was brought into this world to do. That is how it feels to be in harmony with the voice of the soul.

Conversely, moments of depression or "heaviness of spirit," as Rav Kook puts it, may surface when we do not listen to this voice. "Toxic stones gather around one's heart." Something seems to be missing, something is just not right. Outwardly, it may seem that you are succeeding in your life. There is no apparent crisis, but something is lacking. Even if you are not tuned to this "soul station," it is still broadcasting, the feeling of depression is one of its messages. When your body hurts, the message is: "Pay attention, something is not right." The pain is a symptom, a wake-up call that something needs to be changed. Likewise, a moment of dejection may be a symptom, a sign from the soul that something needs attention. Something needs repairing.

It is not simple to listen to this voice, to open up to a spiritual lightning bolt. In fact, it may prove to be the most courageous act of your life.

During my first year of teaching, a student with little religious background joined my class. An actress by profession, this woman had grown up disconnected from Judaism, yet for some reason felt the need to deepen her knowledge. The year of learning began, and she flourished. Her presence illuminated the whole school. Because of her training as an actress, she had no problem memorizing entire sections of the Talmud. Her glow became more luminous as the year progressed. She was discovering her spiritual identity, and all around her – teachers and students alike – benefited from her gentle radiance. One day in November, she asked to speak with me privately. We went outside and sat down on the grass.

"I have to leave," she told me.

I was stunned. Out of all the students in the program, she was the last person from whom I expected to hear this. "Why?"

"I've decided that I need to get a Ph.D., and I need to start studying for it during the January semester."

"Getting a Ph.D. is a long process," I replied. "Probably five years at least. Does it make such a difference if you start in January or wait till next fall?"

She paused. "Well, it is not really the Ph.D. I really need to spend more time with my family."

"Where is your family?"

"Boston."

"Where are you going back to?"

"Arizona."

Then she paused for a long time. I had no idea what to expect, but I saw that she was in anguish.

A few minutes later, she burst out, "I love being here. The learning speaks to the depth of my soul in a way that nothing else has. But I have to leave. I do not know what will happen to me if I stay and I am afraid of that." She began to cry. Shortly thereafter, she left.

Intelligence may be a great gift, but it can also act as an obstacle to personal clarity and self-knowledge. Sometimes we just think too much, and as a result we lose touch with our sense of intuition. We plague ourselves with questions like: "Is it reasonable? Is it responsible? Is it pragmatic?"

Although I come from a family of thinkers, scientists and philosophers, the crucial decisions I have made have not been the product of rational thought and reasoning. The important decisions have resulted from moments of intuition – a sense, a spiritual moment – in which everything suddenly became clear. I could not have explained or rationalized these moments to anyone, least of all to myself. Yet my sense of what to do was completely clear.

What is this moment that Rav Kook refers to as "actual prayer"? It is simply a moment of listening in which one stops thinking and acting, to tune into the voice of the soul. Try to answer the questions: "Who am I? What is my purpose in life? Am I on track?" I am not analyzing my life. I am not emoting or asking for anything. I am simply trying to listen more closely to who I really am.

In truth, this is the primary goal of life – to listen to the voice of one's soul and to act accordingly. "All of one's efforts to learn Torah and acquire her wisdom is to enable the concealed prayer of the soul to be revealed." According to Rav Kook, this personal knowledge is always within reach. Pause and listen to your own spiritual heartbeats.

Summary:

Prayer invites you to listen to the voice of your soul, a voice that is always broadcasting. Your soul is sending the message that you can and should realize your potential in this world and that you have all the unique God-given gifts you need to do so.

Bringing the Godfile into your life:

As you become more receptive to your deepest spiritual voice, you will also become more attuned to the deeper, more spiritual, voice of others. As you understand that you have a unique contribution to make in this world, so too will you learn to recognize the singular gifts of others. You will acknowledge that social pressures to conform can dull your awareness of the special qualities you and others have to offer the world.

A relationship guided by the Listener's approach will focus on creating a space of silence in which each partner can really hear the other. "Toxic stones" can also gather around the heart of a relationship, creating a sense that something is missing and lacks vitality. This too may be a wake-up call instructing you to devote more attention to the relationship, to listen more carefully with the goal of reinvigorating the unique dimensions of this friendship.

Listening creates a space that allows the uniqueness of each relationship – including your relationship with God – to emerge. It encourages each of us to have the openness and strength required to listen to our individual voices, and the courage to open the door for our angel. By doing so, we will discover perpetual opportunities for self-renewal as well as for the renewal of all relationships.

Everything that is true like this \|\| *is also true like this* ⇌.

The Listener – A Spiritual Check-Up

1. Have I ever experienced a moment in which I heard the "continual prayer of my soul"? Have I ever experienced moments of depression because I was not being true to my deepest self?

2. How would my life be different if I listened more intently to my inner voice?

3. What is holding me back from listening more to the voice of my soul?

4. The person I know who listens the most deeply is _____.

5. The person who needs me to listen more intently to him or her is _____.

The Talker

It is essential to make time every day to seclude one-self and talk openly to God. *Speech has great power to awaken a person spiritually.* If he expresses himself with many words of spiritual awakening, entreaties and prayer, this speech itself will bring revelation and an awakening of his soul. Meditation should consist of conversation with God. One should pour out his thoughts before his Creator. This can include complaints and excuses, or words seeking grace, acceptance and reconciliation. There will be many times when one will find it impos-sible to say anything. His mouth will be sealed, and he will not be able to find any words to say. Nevertheless, the very fact that he has made the effort and has pre-pared himself to converse with God is in itself very beneficial. Actually, one can make a conversation and prayer out of this itself. He should cry out to God that he cannot even speak.

*Rebbe Nachman from Bratslav**

Three steps backward, three steps forward. You are alone with yourself. What are you thinking?

"Speech has great power to awaken a person spiritually."

You simply start to talk. You are not thinking, loving, or trying to have a mystical experience. You begin wherever you may be at that moment. This is your rendezvous with God. There is no agenda. There is no plan. There are no expectations or time limits. Lately, you have not had a chance to converse with God, so now is the time. There are no distractions or pressing demands that require your attention. You are not reciting the words of the prayerbook or someone else's words. Your words are your own. You talk about whatever is on your mind – whether you want to ask for something, express gratitude, share or vent.

At the beginning of our marriage, my wife would occasionally mention that she was going out to lunch to talk with one of her girlfriends. I would inevitably ask, "Oh, is anything wrong?"

"No, we are just going to have lunch and talk."

"What do you need to talk about? What is on your mind?"

"Nothing is wrong. We are just going out to talk."

The conversation would often leave me confused – I was

---

* Rebbe Nachman of Bratslav, *Likutei Maharan*, Chassidei Bratslav Publishing, Jerusalem, 1981, Part II, Chapter 52 (author's translation).

unable to fathom what exactly would take place when my wife met her friend. What did they hope to accomplish? What issue was troubling my wife so much that she needed to meet her friend for lunch?

I imagine that the answer is obvious to most people, but it took me years before I understood what really happened when my wife and her friends would go out for lunch: they would have an open-ended, non-goal-oriented conversation. The conversation would emerge through its own natural process. By simply talking, the women would forge a deeper connection, and would ultimately achieve a deeper understanding of themselves and each other.

How do I do talk to God? Certainly not by focusing on the past, engaging in a retrospective examination of my life, or on future plans. At this moment, I am completely focused on the present. Sometimes we censor our words and thoughts, carefully preparing them in our heads before we speak. Conversations end up resembling term papers. But right now, I am not concerned with the structure or the clarity of my words. What concerns me is, "Where am I right now? What is going on with me? What is on my mind?"

I once asked several students to experiment with this form of praying. Their assignment was to find a time and place where they would be free of any distractions. They were to engage in this exercise regardless of their hesitations or ambivalence about their belief in God. In addition, they could not just think their own private thoughts – they had to speak out loud.

One student did the exercise on her porch late at night. Another woke up at two in the morning to try it. A third found an empty classroom. Ostensibly, what could be easier? There would be no one around to correct them, judge whether their words were trivial or profound, mundane or spiritual.

All they had to do was to open their mouths and begin talking. This was their opportunity to conduct a private, secret rendezvous with God.

Amazingly, each of the students reported a similar experience. When they first began to talk out loud, they felt self-conscious. But within five minutes, they all found themselves crying. They were not sure why, but left alone to converse with God, each soon became overwhelmed with emotion.

Here is Kate's description of her experience:

I was daunted about how to start, so I began by recounting a dream I had the night before, trying to figure out what it meant. Then I began talking about the ambivalence I was feeling at that moment – was I just talking to myself in a room, or was God really listening? And even if God were listening, could God answer? Could I understand that answer?

The dream was about my brother dying, and I started getting really angry... I started putting a voice to that and really yelled at God, getting very upset. I started crying. And that really gave expression to something I had felt for a long time, which was that I do believe in God, but that I am very angry with God. That is just where I was. So I screamed and I cried and I talked about all the things that bothered me, all the things I had been thinking about lately.

It came in waves for me, each about 20 minutes of continuous flowing talk, with a moment of silence in between them where I caught my breath. Afterwards I felt pretty calm, that special calmness that comes after crying. At the end I knew I was finished because no more words came, and I just sat in the room for a long time until I felt like I was alone again.

What had happened to Kate? To the others?

Their talking had brought them to an unexpected place. While doing this exercise, they were totally focused on the present moment. There were no distractions, and there was no one else to concentrate on or interact with. At that moment, they were completely focused on themselves and their relationships with God.

The fact that they were talking – or supposed to be talking – to God made them feel as if they were standing before a mirror of truth. At the same time they were talking and listening to themselves. They articulated their fears and their dreams, opening up to themselves in the deepest way. There is a saying, "Words that come out of one's heart go into another's heart." Sometimes, that "other" may even be God. Or it may even be oneself.

While this approach is extremely valuable in developing a vibrant relationship with God, it is difficult to bring into the *Amida*, the silent standing prayer. It is hardly appropriate to begin talking aloud while the entire congregation is standing in silence. Nevertheless, during this time it is possible to carry out a silent conversation in one's mind. It is possible to allow one's thoughts to flow freely for a few minutes, and then to reflect on what this free-flowing expression revealed.

Summary:

Prayer is a conversation which allows your thoughts and words to flow naturally and chart their own course. This process enables you to clarify what you are truly thinking about God at that moment. You may discover what is residing deep within your heart.

Bringing the Godfile into your life:

As you become more comfortable talking in stream-of-consciousness mode to God, so too you may find it easier to converse similarly with your friends.

Talking does not only involve *expressing* your thoughts or feelings. It may also involve *discovering* those thoughts or feelings. This approach allows you to talk without the pressure that accompanies a goal-oriented conversation. Words can still be spoken even if they do not bring a resolution. There can be words that deepen your understanding of relationships, and ultimately yourself.

This form of communication, which does not target any specific issues, allows for free and open exchange. The sentences do not necessarily flow smoothly, and the thoughts do not need to be carefully crafted and developed. You are not writing an essay, and there is no grade.

Often when I get together with friends, one of the first questions asked is, "How are you doing?" How does one answer this question? Do I *know* how I am doing? Can I find the answer to this question in a moment or two, in a sentence or two? The Talker's approach to prayer allows you to focus on the present moment. "How *are* you doing?"

Just as open-ended talking during prayer can evoke and reveal a deeper understanding of your relationship with God, so can this form of expression be a vehicle for discovering the depths of your interpersonal relationships. When you are free from the burden of having to craft complete, logical and carefully constructed thoughts, there is an enhanced probability that you will strengthen your relationships through stream-of-consciousness connecting.

Everything that is true like this ↑↓ is also true like this ⇄.

The Talker – A Spiritual Check-Up

1. Have I ever had a stream-of-consciousness conversation with God? When?

2. How would my life be different if I found a few minutes each day to talk privately with God?

3. Why is it sometimes hard for me to talk directly to God?

4. Have I ever discovered something about a relationship or myself through stream-of-consciousness talking?

5. Who allows me to talk so that I do not feel the need to censor my words or feel self-conscious? Do I do this for anyone?

The Servant

The only meaning of prayer as a religious institution is service of God by man who accepts the yoke of the kingdom of Heaven… Only the prayer which one prays as the observance of a *mitzvah* (religious obligation) is religiously significant. Spontaneous prayer, which a person prays of his own accord, is permitted by Jewish law, but its religious value is small. Moreover, it is of a suspicious quality, since he who prays for the purpose of satisfying his needs makes himself an end, and God, as it were, a means to himself. *The greatness and power of prayer, the legally mandated fixed and obligatory prayer, is in the rejection by man of all personal interests and motives…* in favor of the awareness of standing before God, a posture which is identical to all people in all conditions and in all circumstances, and is not dependent on one's personal history or what has occurred to him; i.e., the extinction of a person's will in favor of the obligation to serve God.

*Professor Yeshayahu Leibovitz**

Three steps backward, three steps forward. You are alone with yourself. What are you thinking?

"The greatness and power of prayer, the legally mandated fixed and obligatory prayer, is in the rejection by man of all personal interests and motives."

Out of all of the approaches discussed within these pages, my students have experienced the most difficulty with this approach to prayer.

In this approach, you are rejecting all personal interests and motives. You are neither judging yourself nor expressing your love for God. You are neither focused on talking to God nor on listening to the inner voice of your soul. Now you are completely absorbed in the act of fulfilling God's command. You are performing this act of prayer because you are obligated to do so. You have utterly disassociated your personal world from the act of praying. You have nullified your personal voice.

Why are you praying? You are praying because you are commanded to pray. Performing the will of God is your sole objective. If you seek to derive personal meaning, clarity or spiritual value from this act, then you are diluting its religious essence. Your prayer would then become an action done for you, not for God. This form of prayer is not an outlet for the

---

* Professor Yeshayahu Leibovitz, *Judaism, Human Values, and the Jewish State,* edited and translated by Eliezer Goldman, Harvard University Press, Cambridge, Massachusetts, 1992, p. 30.

stirrings of the heart or for the meditations of the mind. Your own concerns will have to wait.

This approach to prayer is seemingly the antithesis of what one would expect prayer to be. It is devoid of all personal goals or qualities. While seeking a connection with God might seem to be a primary objective in prayer, in this approach, the more the "I" is involved in the act, the less of a connection there is.

Concentrating on personal goals during prayer can reduce the act of worshiping God to an act of self-service. If you are requesting something from God – even though you may profess to be serving God while doing so – are you not using God as a *means* to satisfy your own desires? If you are praying with the hope that you will feel more at peace with yourself, if you expect to feel more connected, more elevated or pure through prayer, then whom is this moment really for? Is the goal of prayer to make myself feel better?

When prodded with these questions, my students sometimes verge on rioting as they struggle to control their visceral responses of frustration and anger. Challenging questions begin to erupt, such as: "Does this mean that I am supposed to be a robot, mindlessly reciting the words? What about Hannah's prayer asking to have a child, or Moses's plea to enter into the land of Israel? Didn't they have a personal interest in their prayers?" Following these initial outbursts, mumbled comments can sometimes be heard: "This is exactly why I hated prayer in Sunday School. This seems so empty to me. I couldn't do this for two days before looking for another religion."

After allowing the students time to express their hostile feelings, I asked them to consider two scenarios.

First Scenario: Imagine that you are in a long-term relationship with someone, a relationship of trust and caring. One day, your partner asks you to do something. The request makes a lot of sense to you. You say to yourself, "That is a really good idea. I am happy to do that. In fact, I wish that I had thought of it myself." Then you go ahead and do what your partner requested.

Second Scenario: The same partner asks you to do something. The request strikes you as absurd. Why on earth would he or she want me to do this? The request is neither difficult nor unfeasible. It just does not make any sense to you. For a brief moment, you think to yourself that your partner is crazy, wasting your time. But you say to yourself, "I would never have thought or chosen to do this, and what's more, I really do not see the value in it, but because my partner really wants me to do it, I will do it. I'll do it just because my partner asked me to do it."

Then I asked the students, "Of these two scenarios, which one speaks more about the level of commitment and dedication to the relationship?" They paused, reluctant to say something positive about this type of approach to prayer, but they understood the point. The fact that I would do something solely to satisfy my partner's desire, however irrational it may be, indicates the depth of my commitment to the relationship. My commitment to the relationship supersedes my own personal needs or feelings.

This is the Servant's approach to prayer. Why am I praying? I am praying because God wants me to pray. What am I getting out of this act? My growth is not the issue here, because this prayer is not for myself. It is a reflection of my commitment to the relationship. I am doing what I am supposed to be doing.

Eventually, one student spoke up. "You know, I can appreciate this approach," he began. "While other approaches may seem more uplifting or more meaningful, there are many times when I just do not feel like being introspective or spiritual. I am too tired, distracted, or just not in the mood. There are times when I just pray because that is what I am supposed to do."

Summary:

This approach to prayer invites you to express your total dedication to your relationship with God, and to understand that God is the source of the command to pray.

Bringing the Godfile into your life:

As you learn to reject or minimize personal interests and motives in prayer, you will also learn to minimize personal interests and motives in your relationships. Social structures supersede personal needs. The demands of family, community and nation assume pre-eminence in life. Personal needs are subjugated to the greater good of the larger group.

This approach to God and human relationships focuses on your level of dependability and loyalty; your own mood, needs and desires are not central.

This approach epitomizes what we might characterize as a good neighbor: someone who is totally dependable and reliable. If your friend needs something to be done, don't ask questions and examine motives. Just do it. Regardless of what is going on in your personal life, make sure your friend knows that you can be counted on. There are no extenuating circumstances. For the moment, personal interests are put into abeyance. Focus on the job at hand, on the needs of the other, and this attitude ultimately will form the basis for a solid relationship.

Everything that is true like this ⇅ is also true like this ⇌.

The Servant – A Spiritual Check-Up

1. Are there things that I do in my religious life because I think that they ought to be done, without thinking of my own personal needs or possible gain from such actions?

2. Do I ever wonder if I am doing an act for God or for my own benefit?

3. How would I characterize my level of dependibility?

4. Who is the most dependable person that I know, the person who will come through for me regardless of personal mood or situation?

5. When was the last time that I did something for someone solely because the person wanted or needed it to be done?

The Sufferer

Prayer in Judaism is bound up with the human needs,
wants, drives and urges which make man suffer. Prayer is
the doctrine of human needs. Prayer tells the individual, as well as the community, what his, or its, genuine
needs are, what he should, or should not, petition God
about... Who prays? Only the sufferer prays... To the
happy man, to the contented man, the secret of prayer
was not revealed. God needs neither thanks nor hymns.
He wants to hear the outcry of man, confronted with
a ruthless reality.

Suffering or distress, in contradistinction to pain,
is not a sensation, but an experience, a spiritual reality
known only to humans...Whenever a merciless reality

clashes with the human existential awareness, man *suffers* and finds himself in distress.

Rabbi Joseph B. Soloveitchik*

Three steps backward, three steps forward. You are alone with yourself. What are you thinking?

"Prayer in Judaism is bound up with the human needs, wants, drives and urges which make man suffer."

What are your needs? Are you suffering?

"Only the sufferer prays…man suffers and finds himself in distress."

What is this suffering? What is this distress?

There are many questions that people ask each other when they meet for the first time: "Where are you from? What do you do? Where do you live?" But if there were only one question that could be asked, what would it be? What question would reveal the essence of that person? Perhaps it would be: "What are you yearning for?" Rav Soloveitchik once remarked that you can tell a lot about a person by how he or she prays. If you know what a person yearns for and dreams of, if you know how he or she envisions an ideal world, then you have discovered the essence of that person.

When your present reality clashes with your yearned for reality, you suffer. This suffering is not a momentary feeling that comes and goes. This suffering represents a state of being. The extent of the gap between your ideal state and actual reality is what determines the degree of suffering. If there is only a small difference between the envisioned ideal and the actual

---

* Rabbi Joseph B. Soloveitchik, Tradition Magazine, vol. 17, #2, Spring 1978, pp. 57, 65, 66.

situation, then your suffering is slight. If, however, there is a great disparity between them, your suffering is considerable.

Once in class, I read aloud a story, "Bontshe the Silent," written by the Yiddish writer I.L. Peretz. Bontshe was a poor man who led a miserable life, not experiencing much joy or fulfillment. At the end of the story, Bontshe, upon his arrival in heaven, is allowed to ask for anything he wants. He cannot believe his good fortune. In astonishment, he asks the heavenly tribunal again and again, "*Anything* I want?" "Yes," they reply, "anything you want." "Well then," says Bontshe, "I would like hot rolls with butter every morning." The angels then drop their heads in shame and Satan throws his head back and laughs.

In class, we discussed the story at length. The students analyzed the end of the story, and came to the conclusion that Bontshe was so trapped in the smallness of his life that he had lost the ability to dream of something greater than hot rolls with butter. He could have asked for so much – world peace or the Messiah – but he could not see past his own shrunken reality. The story painfully demonstrates how people can be so limited by their physical existence that they cannot conceive of anything greater.

We had finished our discussion, and I was about to continue with the day's lessons when an elderly gentleman, Micha, raised his hand. We were all surprised because we knew that he had a terrible stutter. It would sometimes take him several minutes before he managed to utter a single word. He had been present in the class all year, but this was the first time he had raised his hand. In fact, he had never spoken in any of his classes. I called on him to speak.

Micha opened his mouth, and we waited patiently for several minutes, interspersed with lengthy delays, as he desperately struggled to force out each word. Finally, he spoke: "I am an old man, and my time before the heavenly tribunal is approaching. I have often thought about what I will say, what I will ask for. If I had only one wish, I would ask for Heaven to grant me the ability to talk without the agony of stuttering. Is that a 'small' request? Am I just like Bontshe?"

The whole class sat in stunned silence. This man, who had just spoken now for the first time in class, had expressed his deepest fear in front of students, many of whom were fifty years younger than himself.

After a prolonged silence, I asked him, "Micha, why do you desire to talk freely?"

"I would like to talk," he replied slowly. "If only I could talk, then I think I could do more to make this world a better place."

The entire class smiled. And Micha smiled too. There was no need to respond; we all understood. Micha's request was by no means small. In fact, it was drawn on the largest canvas possible, the healing of the whole world.

What is the source of suffering? Why the anguish?

The immediate goal of delving into suffering is not to find a solution to the chronic problems of the world. During this moment of prayer, you are not seeking a way to alleviate the world's suffering, nor are you searching for practical or behavioral results. Rather, you are deepening your awareness of the freedom that lies within you to improve the situation. Each individual is free – both physically and existentially – to change his or her reality. Victims of slavery often do not even imagine that they can change their reality. Similarly, if we resign ourselves to our present reality, if we cease to imagine that we have the potential to change, then we have become slaves of our own making. The feeling of suffering is thus transformed into an act of independence. It means that you can contemplate a reality that is different from the one in which you presently exist. It means that you refuse to accept the limitations of today's reality.

When you adopt the approach of the Sufferer, you bask in your suffering. Though you may personally be enjoying a wonderful life, the awareness that others are not so blessed impacts your whole being. The Sufferer's prayer reflects existential angst at living in an incomplete world, an unredeemed world. It is a rejection of the "don't worry, be happy" approach to life. There is no medication that can alleviate the pain of this suffering. Rather, it reaches the core of your personality, determining how you experience the world. Numbing yourself to this source of distress would be tantamount to becoming indifferent to the pain of others.

Although the Sufferer does not necessarily aim to change his or her behavior through this approach, the deepening of this acute heartache can catalyze personal and social growth. The experience of suffering is not intended to depress or emotionally paralyze the sufferer. On the contrary, the greater your awareness of the suffering in the world, the greater will be your motivation to narrow the gap between the ideal and the real.

Summary:

This approach to prayer invites you to experience the anguish of the imperfect reality we live in, and in so doing, to deepen your yearning and motivation for change.

Bringing the Godfile into your life:

As you begin to sensitize yourself to the flaws of this world, you will also learn to recognize the shortcomings of your own personality and relationships. As you envision a picture of an ideal world, you will begin to imagine how your relationships could ideally appear. You will no longer live in denial, pretending that everything is in place when there is actually work to be done. You will feel the weight of responsibility for improving your relationships, since even the best relationships need to be continually revisited and deepened.

This awareness, this state of suffering, should not turn you into a "black cloud" spreading gloom, and should not be confused with despair. In fact, quite the opposite is true. Since you are now more acutely aware of the potential hidden within each relationship, you are filled with greater optimism and hope for change. The state of suffering is a statement of protest: today's reality does not have to be the reality of tomorrow. Anguish is both a rejection and a protest. It is a rejection of the concept of a fairy-tale world that requires no change. It is a protest against the idea that change is impossible to achieve. This approach serves as the basis for all human relationships.

Everything that is true like this ↑↓ is also true like this ⇌.

The Sufferer – A Spiritual Check-Up

1. How would I characterize my level of suffering regarding the gap between an ideal world and the present reality?

2. How would my life be different if I yearned more deeply for a better world?

3. What is holding me back from sincerely yearning for more?

4. With which relationship have I become complacent? How could I raise my expectations of this relationship?

5. With which aspect of my life have I become complacent?

The Malcontent

Good morning to You, Lord, Master of the Universe. I, Levi Yitzhak, son of Sarah of Berditchev, I come to You with a complaint from Your people Israel. *What do You want of Your people Israel?*

Rebbe Levi Yitzhak of Berditchev [*]

Three steps backward, three steps forward. You are alone with yourself. What are you thinking?

I am angry. I am angry at God. I have a complaint: "God, what do You want from Your people?!"

---

[*] Rebbe Levi Yitzhak of Berditchev, *The World of a Hasidic Master: Rabbi Levi Yitzhak of Berditchev,* Jason Aronson, New Jersey, 1994, p. 86.

Do not ignore or deny your feelings. Prayer should be personal, it should be authentic, and for the Malcontent, it is. Now is not the time to demonstrate piety or calmness. This moment of encounter should be as sincere and truthful as possible.

The anger is bubbling inside you. Words come out in torrents. "Have You answered our prayers? Have You helped us? Look at what is happening to us!" Anger and accusations are expressed. Disappointments and frustrations are vented. The rage is bursting out. Don't be a martyr. Refuse to accept everything that happens! What kind of relationship is this?!

Is the approach of the Malcontent healthy? Is it not somewhat heretical?

How does a person come to terms with anger toward God? It hurts so much. Do you wish to continue this relationship, to work through this anger? Or is it preferable to remain angry?

The greatest danger to a relationship is the severing of all communication. The pain is too great to bear, so silence sets in. "It hurts too much to talk about it. How could you do this to me? I do not want to talk about it at all." Silence can destroy a relationship in the same way that cancer slowly destroys the human body. When a relationship suffers from a breakdown in communication, it eventually dies.

Conversely, the expressing of pain and anger can help a relationship recover. Despite it all, talk. Despite it all, continue. No silence, not even during the hardest of times.

What is the source of anger at God? Perhaps you are angered at the latest series of events that have befallen the Jewish people. We have certainly suffered our share of calamities. "Why did You let this happen?!" Scream out, knowing that there is no answer, that there will never be an answer. Know that God's ways are beyond human comprehension. But call out nonetheless. Why? What's the point? Because there cannot be silence in the face of tragedy.

A response would be welcome, but do not expect a heavenly voice to miraculously respond to pleas and accusations. Rage against God is an act of protest that keeps you from becoming immune to pervasive pain. One cannot simply accept the misfortune of others. When life's events are beyond comprehension, it is only through protest that a relationship with God can be maintained.

Sometimes I get angry over the greater issues, issues regarding the Jewish people and the world. But other times, my anger stems from personal frustrations and disappointments. "Why did this happen to me? Why did this happen to my child, to my work, to my things?"

Sometimes, when I express my anger over personal frustrations, I achieve a moment of insight, realization, and acceptance. "Ahh." The world does not function according to my desires or timetable. It would be wonderful if the world did adhere to my plans. But in the process of listening to myself express anger, I come to recognize that my annoyance stems, at least in part, from my lack of control. My anger is, to a degree, self-serving, granting me a momentary sense of control over a situation which has, until now, escaped me.

A plan is unfolding, but not the one I had in mind. Once I understand that no simple or miraculous solutions will cure my crises, that the sea will not part and that the sun will not stand still, I begin to realize that my fury stems from a flawed expectation – that I should be in complete control of my life, and that everything should unfold according to my own plan.

By expressing anger, you may begin to accept the fact that you cannot have total control over your life, and that you are subject to countless forces which defy human comprehension.

Accepting this lack of control not only helps you to maintain a relationship with God, but also to solidify it. Incomprehensible, unfathomable things happen. This realization does not give you an excuse to take a passive role in your life, but it may be a catalyst to adjust expectations.

Don't be stoic. Ask yourself:

- How much of my anger stems from my own desire to be in control?
- How much of my frustration is the inevitable result of my false sense of personal power?
- Do I need to adjust my expectations?

Summary:

This approach to prayer invites you to recognize and express your anger, thus preventing a malignant silence from slowly destroying your relationship with God. It is an opportunity to express sadness and outrage over tragedies and disappointments in life. Furthermore, this type of prayer invites you to adjust your expectations in life, preventing a total breakdown in your relationship with God.

Bringing the Godfile into your life:

Just as you cannot allow your relationship with God to deteriorate into self-destructive silence, the same is true for your interpersonal relationships. Every relationship experiences difficult periods of resentment and frustration. Sometimes anger can even, paradoxically, provide you with a certain sense of pleasure. Ask yourself, "Do I want this relationship to continue, or do I prefer to wallow in my anger and pain?"

Several years ago, our landlord knocked on our door and told us that he was going to double our rent. We had three little kids at the time and my wife was eight months pregnant with our fourth. We had lived in the apartment for three years, cultivating what we had thought to be a warm relationship with the landlord. Out of the blue, he informed us: "I am sorry, but we cannot be sentimental over these things." Outraged and burdened with the pressure of packing up all our belongings, we were frantic to find a new place.

I never spoke to our landlord again. For months afterward, I boiled with rage, fantasizing about how one day I would get even with him. Now I look back on this incident with a sense of loss. I never directly expressed to him how I felt, neither at the time nor afterward. Perhaps there was a reason for his behavior. Instead of confronting him and expressing my anger, I remember the sweet pleasure I took in thinking how one day I would repay him in kind.

The Malcontent's approach to prayer teaches you to confront that painful reality head-on and to deal with it. Otherwise, the relationship will wither away.

In addition, the reason for your anger may become clearer once it is expressed. Why are you getting angry? Is it justified? Is the other person really to blame in this circumstance, or does it have more to do with the fact that you have unrealistic expectations? Venting anger may result in a new awareness of the other. Maybe that person does not want to or cannot change at this time. Maybe you need to accept the other's limitations. Maybe anger was the result of unrealistic expectations, and in order to heal the relationship, you need to adjust these expectations.

Everything that is true like this ↑↓ *is also true like this* ⇌.

The Malcontent – A Spiritual Check-Up

1. If I am angry at God, do I express this in words or in silence? When was the last time I voiced my anger toward God?

2. If I were to lash out at God now regarding an issue concerning the Jewish people, what would I say?

3. If I were to scream at God now regarding a personal issue, what would I say?

4. Which relationship have I allowed to fade away instead of choosing to openly communicate my anger?

5. Has expressing my anger ever helped to heal a relationship?

The Needful

It is the need alone that God considers... Jewish prayer covers every area of human life, the material as well as the spiritual, the personal as well as the social, the national as well as the universal. Jewish prayer shows no less appreciation of moral and spiritual values than some of the most significant tomes of the philosophers, yet a Jew prays unabashedly for his daily bread as well as for the needs of the spirit.

*Rabbi Eliezer Berkovits**

* Rabbi Eliezer Berkovits, *Studies in Torah Judaism – Prayer,* Yeshiva University Department of Special Publications, New York, 1962, pp. 23, 26.

Three steps backward, three steps forward. You are alone with yourself. What are you thinking?

"It is the need alone that God considers."

What could be easier than asking for something I need? Children do it endlessly: "Can you please give me this, can you please give me that?"

On the surface, entering into this mindset appears to be easy and uncomplicated. We do not have to engage our deepest thoughts or emotions. In fact, there is very little we have to do. All we have to do is ask.

But in actuality, for most of us, asking for what we need is no simple task. It is not easy to admit that we cannot satisfy our own needs, to accept that we have to look elsewhere for assistance. An essential part of adulthood is moving from a state of dependence to a state of independence. As children, we depend wholly on others to satisfy our needs while dreaming of the day when we will become self-sufficient. The need to ask means we have reverted to a state of childhood dependence. It is an admission that we cannot fully take care of all of our needs.

In this form of prayer, you flood God with your requests. "God, please grant me good health, success at work, a partner in life, children, etc."

When discussing this approach with my students, they often comment: "But, isn't this approach just an invitation to become a 'nudge'? Doesn't this approach encourage you to sit back and ask God to do all of the work? What about striving to fulfill one's own needs?"

Asking God for help does not absolve you from working to achieve your goals. Rather, imploring God for help after you have struggled independently is a statement about human frailty. No one can be completely self-sufficient in this world. There will never come a day when people will not need to ask for something.

"It is the need alone that God considers."

Why, of all things, would God want to hear your needs?

It is difficult, even embarrassing, to recognize your essential state of incompletion, to acknowledge your inability to supply everything that you and your loved ones need. When you ask for something, you are admitting weakness, and exposing your vulnerability. While striving to become more successful, powerful and self-reliant, to whom do you dare admit weaknesses? To whom can you admit, "I really need this, can you help me? I really want to provide for my loved ones, but I am not succeeding." To whom? Only to your closest confidante. Only to the one who would embrace you during this moment of confession and would not judge you negatively for your insufficiency. Even with your closest confidante, can you always be so open, so vulnerable?

Three steps backward, three steps forward. You are alone with yourself. What are you thinking?

Your relationship with God is so close and supportive that you can express your deepest needs without constraint or embarrassment. God is your closest confidante.

The true test of an intimate and supportive relationship is whether you are able to share your weaknesses and vulnerabilities. What is the depth or quality of a relationship in which you cannot ask for something? In which nothing is asked of you?

In this approach to prayer, what you ask for is less significant than the fact you asked for it. The very act of asking for help defines, clarifies and transforms the relationship. Your freedom to implore reflects the closeness of the relationship.

It is as if you are saying, "I do not live independently from you. I will never be able to live independently from you. This relationship does not just enhance my life: I need you."

It is clear that many requests uttered in prayer are not answered affirmatively by God. But what happens when a personal need – physical or emotional – or a familial or collective need is granted? If and when your request is fulfilled, how does it make you feel? How do you now relate to improved health, success at work, or finding a partner? Do you now attribute your success to God's affirmative response, and not just a chance occurrence?

The bachelor who prays to find his bride and then meets her feels that his wishes have been granted, that their meeting was not a random occurrence. He perceives an element of "*bashert*," divine intervention, which brought two soul mates together. What might once have seemed as a chance meeting is now understood to be a mysterious act of Divine intervention.

When you ask God for something, your perception of the eventual outcome changes. While you may have done everything in your power to bring about this moment, you now see an element of the Divine in the outcome. This approach transforms your perception of everything in life. Are your accomplishments purely the fruit of your own labors, or has a hidden transcendent force been involved?

When you ask God for something, you are acknowledging your close and personal relationship. Whether these requests are answered or not, you recognize the intimate role that God plays in your life.

Summary:

This approach to prayer invites you to recognize that needs do not reflect inadequacies. Instead, failings offer an opportunity to acknowledge that as a human being, you cannot totally control the events in this world. Dependence is not indicative of failure, but rather invites you to create and develop a relationship with God. In this way, human beings can heighten their sense of appreciation for the hidden, divine nature of the many gifts that we do receive.

Bringing the Godfile into your life:

As you discover that you have needs that you cannot satisfy by yourself, you will become more sensitive to the similar predicament of others. As you express your own weaknesses and vulnerability, you will become more aware of the needs of others. As you become more comfortable asking for help and admitting that you will never be totally independent, you will naturally become more open to others who ask you to help them fulfill their needs and less judgmental of their neediness.

It is difficult to ask for help. Theologian Martin Buber (1878–1965) once remarked that it is easy to answer the question that *is* asked. It is much more difficult to answer the question that is *not* asked. People have needs that are often difficult to articulate.

Those around us may be in need of our help, but reluctant to ask. Your own willingness to ask for help can diminish their hesitation.

The strength of a relationship is measured by the degree of our openness with each other. When you ask a friend for a favor, it reflects the closeness and security you feel in the relationship. Your admission of need may catalyze a similar openness in others, and may even help to create the relationship.

Furthermore, asking someone for something may have less to do with the object at hand and more to do with the relationship itself.

A student of mine, whom I will call Dan, used to say, "May

98 | THE GODFILE

I ask you a question?" whenever he saw me. We never simply talked. We never had a conversation. Rather, there was a one-sided barrage of questions. I began to expect the perpetual, "May I ask you a question? Would you mind if I asked you just one more thing? Can you help me with this issue? Do you mind helping me with this problem?" During the course of the year, the questions became more frequent and quite lengthy. They would come three at a time, then four, then even more. The strings of questions were not connected to each other, and sometimes not even with anything we had studied together.

Eventually I understood that Dan's goal was not to receive answers to his questions. An answer offered would immediately be swallowed up by another question, as if the answer was simply a prelude to the next question. He was not seeking answers – rather he was trying to create a relationship. The questions themselves were simply pretexts for beginning a conversation, for making a connection. It was Dan's way of saying, "Aryeh, I want to talk. I want to be your friend."

Just as you come to realize that hidden, divine processes are involved when you beseech God, you will recognize that your ability to satisfy the needs of another is not the result of a random series of events. Perhaps you will also perceive that there is a mysterious, divine process unfolding which has enabled us to help each other. There may be an element of *bashert* in every encounter.

Everything that is true like this ↑↓ *is also true like this* ⇄.

The Needful – A Spiritual Check-Up

1. How do I feel about myself when I ask God for help?

2. How would my life be different if I felt more comfortable expressing my needs to God?

3. What holds me back from asking for more things? If I were to talk to God now, what would I ask for?

4. Is there any person with whom I feel close enough that I would not hesitate to ask for anything?

5. Who do I think needs something from me but is reluctant to ask for it?

The Artist

The artist may give a concert for the sake of the promised remuneration, but, in the moment when he is passionately seeking with his fingertips the vast swarm of swift and secret sounds, the consideration of subsequent reward is far from his mind. His entire being is immersed in the music. The slightest shift of attention, the emergence of any ulterior motive, would break his intense concentration and his single-minded devotion would collapse, his control of the instrument would fail. Even an artisan can never be true to his task unless he is motivated by love of the work for its own sake. Only by wholehearted devotion to his trade, can he produce a consummate piece of craftsmanship. Prayer, too, is primarily the yielding of the entire being to one goal,

the gathering of the soul into focus… Feeling becomes prayer in the moment in which we forget ourselves and become aware of God… *In prayer we shift the center of living from self-consciousness to self-surrender.*
                                    *Rabbi Abraham Joshua Heschel**

Three steps backward, three steps forward. You are alone with yourself. What are you thinking?

You are the artist. You are totally involved in your art. At a certain point, your own self ceases to exist. Your fingers swarm and seek out the keys, but you no longer direct them. You have given yourself over to the creation of music. There is a force within you that pushes you, impels you and urges you forward. You have become one with the music.

You are no longer the center of your awareness. You have shifted the center of your existence from yourself to something greater. You are simply a channel to bring music into the world. You have subsumed yourself to a greater force. You have willingly surrendered your being to the force of the music. You have shifted your center of being from self-consciousness to self-surrender.

This is the Artist in prayer.

"In prayer we shift the center of living from self-consciousness to self-surrender."

Self-surrender. This is possibly one of the most frightening and intimidating challenges to undertake. Letting go of the "I." You relinquish control, because you are seeking an ultimate connection. "God is the center toward which all forces tend" (Heschel). In order to let God be the center of

---

* Rabbi Abraham Joshua Heschel, *Between God and Man,* Free Press, New York, 1959, p. 201.

your life, you have to yield control. You have to let go of your defense mechanisms and let down your guard. You have to become vulnerable.

The Artist's prayer is not a prayer that involves action or life-affecting decisions. This is not the time for self-judgment or the expression of your needs. You are not loving, talking, dreaming, or even thinking. This is neither a prayer of thanksgiving nor an articulation of a desire. You are neither talking to God, nor seeking to hear God's message. This is a prayer of altered consciousness. The Artist seeks an ultimate connection.

You are on a journey into another reality. While you want to act, contribute and fulfill your destiny in the world, you must first find yourself. In order to find yourself, you need to deeply understand that you are an extension of something greater, of God. Once you have deepened this connection and understanding, you will be able to return to the world with greater dedication, greater clarity and greater peace of mind. You will return with an enriched sense of the "I" from which you took leave during this prayer.

How do I do this? How do I become The Artist in prayer?

Abraham Joshua Heschel came from a *hassidic* line and was certainly familiar with a famous story told by the founder of *hassidism*, the Ba'al Shem Tov. When trying to convey the essence of prayer, the Ba'al Shem Tov related this story:

> There once was a wise and great King, and he built what, for all appearances, seemed like a royal castle with walls and towers and gates. He commanded his people to come through the gates and visit him. He also commanded that, at each gate, treasures of his kingdom be placed. There were those who went as far as the first gate, took

a treasure, and returned home. There were those who continued to the second gate, and then returned home with two treasures. The son of the King *tried very hard to reach his father* [italics added], the King. Then the son saw that, in fact, there were no separations dividing himself and his father. It was all an illusion, all the walls and gates and towers were imaginary.

"The son of the King *tried very hard to reach his father*, the King." The walls did not exist at all. When great effort was made for the sake of the relationship, the walls simply disappeared.

The first step in creating a strong connection with God is desiring the relationship. How seriously do you want this relationship? Does it mean everything to you? Are you willing to open yourself up, to let down your defense mechanisms, and to subsume yourself to the relationship? Are you building walls, or are you ready to say, "I am Yours, God, completely"?

"I am Yours" does not mean that you are relinquishing your physical or emotional self. Rather it means that your center of being, your essence, has shifted. On occasion, I have asked my students how they would answer the question, "Where are you?" One possibility is to answer physically: "I am here. I am in Jerusalem." Or to answer emotionally: "I may look like I am *here*, but my heart is really somewhere else." You might also describe your mental state: "I am not really here. I am thinking about something else."

The Artist answers: "I am Yours. I am on a journey – to the beyond, to the holy, to God. I am allowing my being to be taken over by a greater force which will carry me to an undetermined place. That is what I want more than anything else." Only then, as in the Ba'al Shem Tov's story, will the walls disappear and oneness be achieved.

You do not need to be able to paint, sculpt or play music in order to be an Artist. All that is required is an attempt to become one with the divine creative force of the universe. Artists search for the keys. They do not seek control. They allow a greater force, that sense of the beyond, to surge through them, to enable them to create, to become one with God.

Summary:

This approach to prayer invites you to surrender and subsume yourself to something far greater, to allow your will to become one with God.

Bringing the Godfile into your life:

Each relationship has its own music.

Just as you allow yourself to relinquish control over the process of creating music in your connection with God, so too can you learn to relinquish control over the music of each relationship. There is a dimension of surrender to the relationship. You allow yourself to become vulnerable, to let down your defense mechanisms.

Students have often been aghast at this statement. "Let down my defense mechanisms?!" They have remarked that this is a painful and potentially dangerous practice. This is certainly true. But an artist who struggles to remain in control will never create transcendent music. In the same vein, a relationship which we attempt to control will never reach its potential of infinite beauty.

Every relationship has walls of our own building. We erect walls because we are afraid to cope with another's love, or to maintain the illusion of control. We also build walls to protect ourselves from embarrassment or rejection. In order to become The Artist, the first step is to acknowledge that these walls are imaginary. The next step is to understand the simple truth: that you built them to avoid becoming one with "the other." Just as we build walls that don't exist, so too can we make them disappear.

How often have you said: "I am yours, completely yours"? What does a statement like that say about a relationship? What is holding you back from making such a declaration?

Usually, you are at the center of your life. A moment of surrender, of yielding control, allows the relationship to now become the center of your life.

Everything that is true like this ⇂↾ *is also true like this* ⇌.

The Artist – A Spiritual Check-Up

1. How would I describe my relationship with God vis-à-vis self-consciousness and self-surrender?

2. How would my life be different if I let down the walls between myself and God?

3. What is holding me back from letting down more walls?

4. Whom do I know who most exemplifies the act of self-surrender described by Heschel and the Ba'al Shem Tov?

5. Which relationship of mine contains too many walls? What is holding me back from letting go of these walls?

The Mystic

Do not let your heart fall within you in the erroneous belief that since you have no knowledge of the secret meanings and intentions of the prayers, which cause fixing and repair in the higher realms, your prayers are ineffectual… [Do not say to yourself:] "What use is there in trying to pray with great effort since I do not know how to pray with the kabbalistic [mystical] intentions anyway?" The following example should help you understand why this kind of thinking is mistaken: The watchmaker who fashions the inner workings of a watch knows all the details of its machinery. He is the greatest expert on watches and can fix a watch if it has been broken. Yet anyone is capable of winding the watch. *You do not have to know why winding the watch makes it start ticking; the watchmaker has already set it up so that all you have to do is wind it.* And if you do not wind it, all the watchmaker's labors won't do a bit of good; the clock simply won't run. So it is with prayer.

Rabbi Kalonymous Kalman Shapira*

Three steps backward, three steps forward. You are alone with yourself. What are you thinking?

"You do not have to know why winding the watch makes it start ticking."

I am winding the watch, the watch of the universe.

Just like the watchmaker who made the watch, earlier mystics wrote the prayers. All you have to do is say them. It is all set up for you to put into motion, like winding the watch. "The watchmaker has already set it all up so that all you have to do is wind it."

Mystical prayer is not "I"-focused. You are not thinking about yourself. You are not analyzing or judging yourself. You are not trying to feel the love of God or listen to your deepest voice. It really is not about you at all.

Mystical prayer is focused on penetrating more spiritual worlds, ascending to higher levels of consciousness. In mystical thought, there are four worlds, four different realities. This world is just one of the many worlds created by God, the most physical of the four worlds. There are more spiritual worlds, realities that do not have a physical expression. The mystics refer to these as worlds of angels, seraphim and holy creatures. The mystics desire to experience these worlds and to influence these alternate realities.

---

* Rabbi Kalonymous Kalman Shapira, *A Student's Obligation,* translated by Micha Odenheimer, Jason Aronson Inc., New Jersey, p. 191.

But shouldn't prayer be focused on this world, on you and your life?

The mystics assert that everything in this physical world is really only the expression, the symptom, of what is transpiring in the more spiritual worlds. If you want to correct something in this world, rather than focus on the external symptom, you must try to penetrate the source of the matter in the more spiritual worlds.

For example, if you have a problem in your life, a behavioral psychologist might counsel you to change some element of your behavior. Other psychologists, however, might counsel you not to focus on the external expression of the problem, but rather to go into your subconscious, to discover a deeper source of the problem which has now manifested itself in these particular symptoms. Only by getting to the deeper, more hidden cause will you be able to fully cure yourself.

The mystics use the same reasoning. Only by transporting yourself to the more spiritual worlds can you find a cure for the ailments of this physical world. This journey is accomplished through meditation, and through special prayers of mystical content and intention. You focus your mind and consciousness to detach yourself from your present reality, and enter into an altered state of consciousness through which you hope to arrive at the source of the problem, and then to treat it and heal it.

Often when I teach the approach of The Mystic I find that students completely tune out. They look at me with kind and dispassionate faces, remarking that they have absolutely no idea what I am talking about. After showing them a page in a mystical prayer book, it is clear to me that they neither feel connected to, nor understand, the dynamics of this mystical journey.

In fact, very few of us are mystics. Although small mystical communities and select esoteric groups have practiced these techniques, it is hard for us to fathom what occurs during these mystical encounters. We have not been initiated into this mystical consciousness and do not know how to access these alternate realities. We certainly know little about healing other worlds.

The composers of the Jewish prayer book, however, were aware of these mystical ideas and composed the prayers as a four-stage journey from the most physical world to the most spiritual. Following the order of the prayer book, one first expresses gratitude for the physical body, then moves on to consciousness of the ability to speak, to think, and finally to the world of silence beyond thought. Almost unknowingly, you have been led through the four worlds and have arrived at The Source.

"You do not have to know why winding the watch makes it start ticking. The watchmaker has already set it all up so that all you have to do is wind it."

You can wind the watch. By doing so, you can help turn the gears of the universe.

Even with no understanding of how the watch was made, even though you yourself could never manufacture such a complicated watch, you know how to make it work. The craftsman has fashioned the watch, and all you need to do is wind it.

Prayer is like the watch. The sections of the prayerbook can be compared to the gears of the watch. By saying the prayers, you help wind the universe. You may not understand how it works, and you and I certainly could not have written these prayers. But according to the mystics, saying the words with the proper intention is all that is important. By saying the words, we can sustain the world. The entire world depends on winding the watch properly.

To bring this idea home, I asked my students a series of questions:

First, I asked them if they would feel comfortable delivering a short five-minute speech in class – a speech that they have written, that they think has important educational or moral value. Almost all of them answered that they would be willing to give such a speech in class.

Then I asked them how they would feel delivering the exact same speech in front of the whole school. Many of them responded that they would feel more self-conscious, anxious, and perhaps even afraid.

Then I asked those remaining how they would feel giving the same speech to the whole city. Nervous? They usually gulped hard at this point.

Then I asked them how they would feel giving the exact same speech to the whole country. What if they could have five minutes in which the whole world was linked up to their internet site and they had the attention of everyone in the world? How would they feel giving the same speech in front of the whole world?

Most of them answered that they would probably pass out from anxiety.

Then we discussed why they might feel like this. After all, it was the exact same speech, the exact same words. What difference does it make if I give the speech in front of five, 500 or 500,000 people? It is just me and the words of my speech, the same speech that I gave to the class.

The students responded that they would feel that more people were depending on them, that they would have the weighty responsibility of influencing countless people.

Then we undertook a praying exercise: within the next few days, they all had to try to pray as if the whole world were watching them, listening to them. They were to pray as if they were affecting everyone in the world.

After all, we are winding the watch of the whole cosmos. Prayer is not "I"-focused, or about one person. Rather our prayer affects the whole world and everyone in it.

After attempting this experiment, most students reported that they felt totally drained by the effort. "It was work!" They focused on each word, moving very slowly. Some remarked that they were not able to finish the service. "There's no way that I could do that everyday." One woman noted that she trembled throughout her attempt. Another observed, "I finished long after the whole service was over."

One student remarked that, in general, we are unaware of the power of our prayers, of our potential ability to affect the world. "I may not have mystical powers, and I do not know how to acquire them, but it radically changes my understanding of my potential if I recognize that such powers exist." This knowledge enabled her to appreciate the power she has in her praying and caused her to become more aware of her responsibility to focus on what she was doing.

I have no idea how my e-mail works – I simply press the "send" button and a message is sent across the world. The mystics teach us that the same is true of prayer: by saying certain words we instantaneously send a message across an infinite number of worlds.

Summary:

Mystical prayer invites you to contemplate how words can heal and repair worlds that cannot be grasped by the average human mind. Mystical prayer may even reach the invisible source of this world, with the potential to change and heal the world through the words of the prayerbook.

Bringing the Godfile into your life:

In the same way that you increase your concentration when you imagine that everyone is depending upon your prayer, you can also intensify your focus in each human encounter, as you realize the power of your words. Each person is a whole world.

What would happen to you if you imagine that the whole world was watching you and depended on this conversation?

Just as your prayers can affect an infinite number of worlds – worlds that cannot be seen or imagined – your interaction with a single person may eventually affect a countless number of people in ways that you might never know. Though you may not be conscious of this interconnectedness, each person is a gear of the watch. The ripple effect of each relationship will never be fully known.

Everything that is true like this ↕ *is also true like this* ⇌.

The Mystic – A Spiritual Check-Up

1. If I could talk to the whole world for five minutes, what would I say?

2. Have I ever had a moment which I imagined could influence worlds beyond my immediate reality?

3. Have I ever experienced some kind of mystical connection while using the prayer book?

4. Can you think of any moment in your family's history which affected the whole future family line?

5. Which relationship of mine would benefit if I intensified my focus?

Conclusion

It is difficult to talk about God.

Wherever I go, I find that Jews are reluctant to talk about God. Imagine sitting at a dinner table with your family or friends and saying, "There is something I want to talk about. Can we please talk about God for a while? Can we talk about our relationship with God?" How would you expect people to react? Would they think you were joking? There would probably be an awkward moment of silence, of embarrassment.

For many, talking about one's relationship with God is out of the comfort zone. We are comfortable talking about so many aspects of Judaism – social action, holidays, family, and Israel – yet rarely does God enter into the conversation. We may lead sophisticated lives and be conversant in many subjects, but we are not comfortable with our present understanding of God. Why is that? Perhaps we have not given the subject much thought in our adult lives. Perhaps anything we would have to say on the topic would stem more from our heart than from our mind, and we are uncomfortable revealing ourselves in this way. Perhaps we are embarrassed to discuss something that we sense is terribly profound because we have so little to say on the subject. So we avoid talking about God altogether.

We may attempt to conceal our sense of discomfort by posing good questions, such as, "How can there be a God if there is so much suffering in the world? Where was God in the Holocaust? Is there an ultimate truth?" We have no answers for these questions. So we avoid talking about God.

Rabbi Adin Steinsaltz wrote that the question should not be, "What is God," but perhaps, "What is God to me?" In other words, we may not be able to fathom the mysteries of eternity, but perhaps we can begin to fathom the mysteries of our own souls.

Judaism introduced to the world the belief in a single, supreme God. The first Jew, Abraham, called out in the name of God. Rudolf Otto, the author of the epic theological work, *The Idea of the Holy*, wrote that Jews gave spirituality to the world. My friend Moishe joked that, "Yes, that is exactly the problem. We gave it away to the world. We did not keep any for ourselves!"

Whenever I open a discussion about relationships with God I am greeted with a familiar pattern of reactions. First, a look of astonishment that we are actually talking about this, followed by a sigh of relief and a general release of pent-up frustration. I hear comments such as, "You know, I really do not know if I believe in God or not, but I was uncomfortable talking about it with my rabbi. I felt self-conscious bringing it up. I thought that there was something wrong with me. That I was the only one who felt like this."

How would you answer God's question to Adam and Eve, the very first question in the Torah, *"Ayeka?* Where are you?" Would you hide behind a tree? Would you hide behind words, a joke or a cynical comment? Or could you answer and say "*hineni*," "Here I am." We may be uncertain or unclear about our answers, but we can still be fully present.

Let's begin the conversation. Let's write our own Godfile.

I used to dread going to synagogue. I dreaded going through the motions of prayer. I would seek out the synagogue that prayed at the fastest pace and finished the earliest. I prayed as if under duress, at best as if I were doing a favor to my family or the community, at worst as if prayer were an unwelcome burden to be discharged. Today, while I still continue to experience ups and downs in my spiritual world, I look forward to the opportunity to engage in "the encounter," to click up my Godfile.

Once I was a stranger to my own soul. Writing my Godfile has helped me to find my spiritual path. Using these approaches to prayer has helped to keep it vital and personally meaningful.

I hope that this process will help you as well.

Biographies

Rabbi Eliezer Berkovits (1908–1992)

Rabbi, theologian, passionate philosopher and educator. Born in Romania, he served in the rabbinate in Berlin, Leeds (UK), Sydney and Boston. In 1958, he became chairman of the department of Jewish philosophy of the Hebrew Theological College in Chicago. He relentlessly challenged the modern skeptic to consider the possibilities of a commitment to faith. His writings deal with the contrasting claims of religious tradition and secular nationalism, and include *God, Man, and History* and *Faith after the Holocaust*.

Rabbi Abraham Joshua Heschel (1907–1972)

A descendant of preeminent rabbinic families of Europe. Escaping from the Nazis, he found refuge both in England and America, where he briefly served on the faculty of Hebrew Union College, the main seminary of Reform Judaism. Known as an activist for civil rights in the USA, he is one of the few Jewish writers to be widely read by members of all denominations of Judaism, as well as by many within Christianity. His most influential works include *Man is Not Alone, God in Search of Man*, and *The Sabbath*.

Rabbi Samson Raphael Hirsch (1808–1888)

Rabbi and writer. He was a leading rabbi of Western Europe and leader of the Frankfurt-on-the-Main community for 37 years. He wrestled with the political and cultural challenges that modernity presented to Judaism. His written works include the *The Nineteen Letters*, *Horev*, and commentaries on the Torah and Proverbs. He wrote that all the *mitzvot* (commandments) can be reduced to three basic principles: justice, love, and the education of ourselves and others. Despite considerable opposition to his opinions from many circles in German Jewry, his personal qualities won respect and admiration.

Rabbi Avraham Yitzhak HaCohen Kook (1865–1935)

A rabbinical authority, writer and mystic, he was the first Ashkenazic chief rabbi of modern Israel and spiritual father of the religious Zionist movement. He wrote extensively about the individual's need to unify body and soul, and fulfill one's individual mission within the framework of the Jewish nation. He believed that a divine task had been given to the Jewish people to return to their homeland and create a model spiritual nation. He was a creative thinker who wrote on the Jewish approach to evolution, vegetarianism, art, and virtually every element of modern society.

Yeshayahu Leibowitz (1903–1994)

Born in Riga, educated in Germany and Switzerland, and immigrated to Palestine in 1935. He taught chemistry, physiology, history and philosophy of science at the Hebrew University. He wrote many books and served as an editor of several volumes of the *Encyclopedia Hebraica*. His philosophy of Judaism focused entirely on the importance of Jewish law. Outspoken in his views on Judaism and Israel, his approach sparked a great deal of debate and antagonism among religious and non-religious circles.

Rebbe Nachman of Bratslav (1772–1811)

Creative and controversial *hassidic* leader, originator of Bratslav *hassidism*, and great-grandson of the founder of *hassidism*, the Ba'al Shem Tov. Central to the Bratslav approach was the primacy of belief in God, and spontaneous prayer practices were developed to help foster closeness with the Divine. Rebbe Nachman's works, including *Likkutei Moharan* and stories, sought to bring his *hassidim* to the simple worsh of God. Unlike other *hassidic* dynasties, the Bratslav *hassidim* never chose a replacement for Rebbe Nachman after his death.

Rabbi Kalonymous Kalman Shapira, Rebbe of the Warsaw Ghetto (1889–1943)

One of the central figures of Polish Jewry before and during the Second World War. A descendant of some of the greatest Polish *hassidic* masters, he sought to reignite the *hassidic* fervor of the early masters, thereby combating the increased secularization of the time. He sought to imbue students with a sense of their spiritual potential. Rabbi Shapira did not survive the war. After the war, a volume of the sermons he delivered, *Aish Kodesh* (Holy Fire), was found in the Warsaw ghetto and published.

Rabbi Joseph B. Soloveitchik (1903–1993)

U.S. Talmudic scholar and religious philosopher, and scion of a preeminent Lithuanian rabbinical family. He wrote his doctoral dissertation for the University of Berlin on the epistemology and metaphysics of Hermann Cohen. Rabbi Soloveitchik became the spiritual mentor for the majority of American-trained Orthodox rabbis, and while serving as professor of

Jewish Philosophy at Yeshiva University, inspired students for decades. He wrote of the "covenantal community" that brings God and human beings together in an intimate person-to-person relationship.

R. Levi Yitzhak of Berditchev (1740–1810)

Hassidic leader and rabbi, one of the most famous personalities in the third generation of the *hassidic* movement. He was considered to be the founder of *hassidism* in central Poland. He emphasized the need to serve God with joy and fervent prayer. One of the most beloved of the *hassidic* leaders, he taught that one should not admonish the Jewish people with harsh words, but rather gently, and sought to be a defender of his people. He was known for his interceding with God on behalf of the Jewish people.

Rabbi Shneur Zalman of Liadi (1745–1813)

Founder of Habad *hassidism*. A rabbi and author of legal and *hassidic* writings, he was a great scholar in Talmud and Kabbalah (mysticism). His most famous work, known as the *Tanya*, a systematic explanation of *hassidism*, became accepted as the principal source of Habad philosophy. He stressed that the average person (*beinoni*) should aspire to achieve complete spiritual unity with the Divine with both his emotions and intellect. The struggle to reach higher levels of perfection is dependent on one's ability to enable one's mind to rule one's heart.

About the Author:

Rabbi Aryeh Ben David is the Founder and Director of *Ayeka*: Center for Jewish Spiritual Education. He serves as the Rabbinical Educational Consultant for Hillel International, lecturing throughout the U.S. and internationally, and Director of Spiritual Education and Senior Faculty member of the Pardes Institute in Jerusalem. Rabbi Ben David was also the Educational Director of the Jerusalem campus of Livnot U'Lehibanot. He is the author of the highly acclaimed *'Around the Shabbat Table, A Guide to Fulfilling and Meaningful Shabbat Table Conversations'* (2000 – Jason Aronson). Rabbi Ben David received his Rabbinical Ordination from the Israeli Rabbinate and served in the IDF Artillery Corps. He lives with his wife Sandra and their six children in Efrat, Israel.

Ayeka is an organization dedicated to enabling Jews of all ages and backgrounds to create a deeper personal connection to their Judaism. *Ayeka* has spearheaded a compelling and integrated educational approach that harmonizes the three voices of the soul – the mind, heart, and body (*nefesh*, *ruach*, and *neshama*). Through seminars that integrate intellectual Jewish learning, experiential workshops, and emotive exercises, participants are inspired to lead more meaningful, passionate and caring Jewish lives. See www.ayeka.org.il.

Ex-Library: Friends of
Lake County Public Library